S0-DZO-112

DISCARDED

TAKING YOUR MEETINGS
OUT OF THE DOLDRUMS

Revised Edition

TAKING YOUR MEETINGS OUT OF THE DOLDRUMS

Revised Edition

Eva Schindler-Rainman, D.S.W.
and Ronald Lippitt, Ph.D.

in collaboration with

Jack Cole

Revised by
Eva Schindler-Rainman
with Jack Cole

LAMAR UNIVERSITY LIBRARY

UNIVERSITY ASSOCIATES, INC.
8517 Production Avenue
San Diego, California 92121

AS
6
S318
1988

Copyright © 1975, 1988 by University Associates, Inc.

ISBN: 0-88390-217-6

Library of Congress Catalog Card Number 87-30111

Library of Congress Cataloging-in-Publication Data

Schindler-Rainman, Eva.
    Taking your meetings our of the doldrums/by Eva
Schindler-Rainman and Ronald Lippitt, in collaboration
with Jack Cole.
    —Rev.ed.
    p.   cm.
    Bibliography: p.
    ISBN 0-88390-217-6
    1. Meetings—Handbooks, manuals, etc.
I. Lippitt, Ronald   II. Cole, Jack
III. Title.
AS6.S318 1988
658.4'563—dc19

                                        87-30111
                                        CIP

The materials that appear in this book (except those for which reprint permission must be obtained from the primary sources) may be freely reproduced for educational/training activities. There is no requirement to obtain special permission for such uses. We do, however, ask that the following statement appear on all reproductions.

Reproduced from
Taking Your Meetings Out of the Doldrums
Eva Schindler-Rainman, Ronald Lippitt, and Jack Cole
San Diego, CA: University Associates, 1988

This permission statement is limited to the reproduction of materials for educational/training events. Systematic or large-scale reproduction or distribution (more than one hundred copies)—or inclusion of items in publications for sale—may be done only with prior written permission.

Printed in the United States of America

Interior Design: Mary Kitzmiller
Cover Art: Rob Andreasen

Foreword

There is no possible way to get accurate statistics on the number of meetings held in the world in the course of a year. They take place under such a wide variety of auspices—educational institutions, commercial enterprises, government agencies, voluntary associations—and for such a variety of purposes—learning, planning, negotiating, problem solving, decision making, adjudicating, socializing—that there is no way to keep tabs on them. But certainly they add up to many millions of person-hours annually. In fact, meetings are the principal means of getting human learning and work done.

In view of their importance as instruments of human endeavor it is tragic that most meetings are so bad. The main explanation for this being the case, as I see it, is that traditionally our meetings have followed one or both of two historical models: the lecturer-audience classroom model dating from the medieval school, and the parliamentary model invented by English barons in the thirteenth century. The purpose of both models was to assure that those in power would maintain their control over those under them. Both models are characterized by rigid control by authority figures, formal rules, regulations, and procedures, and standardized rituals.

Perhaps these models served virtuous purposes at the time they were conceived. The classroom model provided an orderly means of transmitting knowledge before printing presses were invented; and the parliamentary model enabled the barons to restrain the tyranny of monarchs without relinquishing power to the vulgar masses. But as the concepts, values, and procedures of democracy began evolving in the late eighteenth century, these models began losing their relevance; and in the twentieth century they became totally dysfunctional.

What was needed was a new model to provide guidelines for human interactions that were more congruent with democratic ideals. To meet this criterion, a new model would need to possess these characteristics: (1) respect for personality, (2) participation in decision making, (3) freedom of expression and availability of information, and (4) mutuality of responsibility for defining goals, planning and conducting programs, and evaluating. Such a model has been emerging. In its educational context it is going under such labels as open learning, self-directed learning, community schools, and the like. In its organizational and political contexts it is going under such labels as participative management, shared management, participative democracy, decentralization, local control, and the like.

But we have had difficulty implementing this new model. Our meetings don't look much different from the way they did in the medieval classrooms and parliaments; decisions still tend to be made by the leadership and passively accepted by the followers. Except that the followers are getting bored and staying away from the meetings at which the leaders announce their decisions.

What has been needed is a new set of tools and procedures for making meetings more participative, for rescuing them from the doldrums. And this is what the authors of this book have assembled from the experience of scores of innovators who have been inventing and trying out new techniques for planning and conducting meetings for a number of years.

What they present here is *not* prescriptions—more rules and regulations—but resources containing principles to stimulate your own innovations and containing optional strategies for you to adapt to your own style. Its key adjectives—involving, stimulating, enjoyable, productive, exciting, motivating, satisfying—describe the kind of meetings you can have if you use its very practical guidelines and tools as resources.

Malcolm S. Knowles
Professor of Adult and Community College Education
North Carolina State University, Raleigh

Contents

Acknowledgments

A special "thank you" for their tremendous help
to the late Ronald Lippitt
and to Thea Key and Barbara Powers.

Introduction

A concern about productive meetings is part of some larger trends and dynamics our society is experiencing. The importance of well-designed meetings and learning events has come to the fore in every sector of society: corporate, voluntary, and government. Indeed it has become important both nationally and internationally for some of the following reasons:

1. There is an increasing emphasis on the full utilization of resources, including money, time, space, materials, environment, and people. There is a great deal of emphasis on the need to decrease polluting the society by misuse of these resources.

2. Increasing attention is being paid to the importance of product and/or effectiveness that can be measured. Most meetings and learning events certainly do not have measurable outcomes as yet.

3. The appropriate and knowledgeable utilization of technology, including the multimedia, is extremely important to planning and leading productive meetings. Indeed, a whole new science could be developed regarding which media are appropriate or inappropriate for various kinds of meetings.

4. The importance of multicultural participation in all parts of the society is certainly being realized. This means that participants in meetings come from a variety of social, cultural, ethnic, and religious groupings with the concomitant differences in belief systems, life styles, and values. These must be taken into account when planning meetings—all the way from the kind of refreshments that are offered to the kind of group participation that is encouraged.

5. It therefore becomes extremely important to accommodate a wide range of value systems. The values that particularly are felt in meetings have to do with time and timing, openness, participative styles, and the use of the English language.

6. There is increasing concern about open and participatory communication and how to make this possible, so that meetings are owned by the participants, and also achieve desired results.

7. Participants are more demanding and expectant in terms of the results of any meeting they attend. Indeed, meeting participants are stating clearly that unless they can participate actively and see the product, there is no need for going to meetings.

8. It is important to handle traditions elegantly. Traditions about meetings, meeting style, and meeting participation are heavily felt in extant organizations. It is time to look at these traditions and decide which are still viable and where change is necessary.

9. The handling of conflict is becoming an important dynamic of many meetings. Therefore meeting leaders need training in how to handle conflict so that it can be a useful, creative dynamic in a meeting, rather than a destructive one.

10. Collaboration is certainly the competence most needed in meetings and learning events. This includes collaboration between disparate players within the organization, as well as collaborative designs and competencies in relation to meetings that include participants from many different systems.

From the above it is abundantly clear that meeting technology is but one of the competencies needed by people who are responsible for designing, planning, and leading meetings, seminars, and other congregate learning events.

Join Us Please!

W e have had an absorbing, and often an "aha" time formulating our experiences about meetings and clarifying how to improve them. Many frustrations have been activated and analyzed. Many ideas that have worked have been integrated into our agenda for sharing with you.

As you can see, the agenda is a full and varied one: full of opportunities for you to add and enrich the wisdom about alternatives for taking all of our meetings "out of the doldrums." The dictionary definition of doldrums, by the way, includes the phrases: "a dull and depressed condition," "the dumps," "a state of inactivity or stagnation," "place in the ocean where baffling calms and winds prevail." These notions sum up many of our experiences about a lot of meetings.

But in contrast, we have all shared the joy of productive, participative meetings where all of us became excited, motivated, lifted up, and committed, because of the sharing and interactions that went on between the participants. Also, these meetings created significant changes in us and made impacts on the larger community.

We are convinced from our own experience that most meetings can be improved a great deal; and all meetings, some. The time spent in using this resource kit, in planning your meetings more effectively, and in training others to plan theirs may be the highest payoff time you will spend as a "people-helper." We don't know of a more rewarding function than being an effective "meeting-helper."

So join us as we:

- identify some of the problems and issues of getting participation in meetings (Unit 1).
- review some of the similarities and differences of all meetings (Unit 2).
- go through the steps of designing all types of meetings (Unit 3).
- use a check list of things to remember in planning and conducting a meeting (Unit 4).
- scan a check list of the kinds of resources there are for use in improving our meetings (Unit 5).
- remind ourselves of the traps we need to avoid in planning and leading meetings (Unit 6).
- have an opportunity to share with you some alternative ways to cope with typical problem situations (Unit 7).
- expand your repertoire with ideas, resources, instruments, and procedures for your meetings (Unit 8).

- help you develop and think about ways to use this resource (Unit 9).
- give you a selected bibliography.

We believe you'll be able to do much about the doldrums and problems in your groups. Improving our meetings is one of the greatest things we can do for ourselves, our groups, our systems, and our democracy.

Eva Schindler-Rainman
Ronald Lippitt
Jack Cole

Revised October, 1987

Unit 1
What This Is All About—and Why and for Whom

Most of the learning and planning and doing of this world happens in groups conducting their activities through meetings. This includes all types of meetings such as seminars, workshops, conferences, classes, etc.

And most of the leaders responsible for helping these groups "do their thing" feel frustrated some of the time or much of the time by the lack of involvement, productivity, excitement, satisfaction, and responsibility-taking by the members of their groups. As chairpersons, teachers, leaders, consultants, officers, they wish the members of their groups would become more "turned on" as learners and more responsible as program participants or planners or action-takers. Meeting participants want more interesting and productive meetings also.

Let's pause a few moments to remind ourselves why it is so often difficult for most of us to become actively involved participants in many of the groups to which we are related.

1. We have been taught, in our growing up groups—the family, the classroom, the Sunday school, etc.—to expect and to wait for initiative and direction from the grownups. They define what is expected, what is okay to do, what would be "graded" as good behavior or good work. It has been safer or polite to wait for somebody else to go first.

2. Many of us have found that the safest way to express our negative feelings about these authority figures is to be non-participative, silent, inactive, withdrawn, and to become bored.

3. We have often subscribed to, or made assumptions about, the way the others in our group feel about active participation and cooperation with the teachers and/or leaders. We assume there would be raised eyebrows or even more active negative feedback if we showed responsiveness, "eager beaver" activity and active involvement in "what they want us to do." Therefore, we inhibit our inclinations to talk back and to test the ideas of the grownups. To do so we assume is dangerous to being accepted by other members.

4. Very few of us have had the exciting experience of belonging to groups that developed and "owned" their own goals, plans and choices of action alternatives.

5. Few of us know alternative ways to design meetings, other than the ones we have seen or been in, even if we'd like to improve them.

So it is really not surprising—although it is still very frustrating—when our groups show less initiative and activity than we hoped for. This may also help to explain some of the priorities for the planning of programs, classes, and meetings and training sessions which we are emphasizing in this resource book. The assumptions here include:

1. Those who are "planned for" as the members or participants in meetings need to have an important part in influencing or participating in the planning, evaluating, and replanning of their own group situation.

2. The members of any group are very different from each other in some aspects of their needs, interests, abilities, and commitments of time and energy to the particular group.

3. Groups differ from one another even if the size, composition and purposes are quite similar.

4. The designs of meetings should invite and provide opportunity for everyone to actively participate, rather than permitting periods of enforced passivity, such as listening to lectures or long reports, or minutes of last meetings, or films.

5. Getting feedback from the member-participants, and utilizing these data for the improvement of the meetings, is one of the most important functions of a good leader or teacher or officer.

So as you scan through these resources and become familiar with where you find what kind of help, you'll see that we have been thinking about the materials and tools and ideas that will help you with all kinds and sizes of meetings in all types of organizations and situations, working with all types of members. You may have a variety of purposes, such as:

• You may want to stimulate more excitement and learning in classes or training sessions.

• You may want to plan interesting, turned-on program activities for the meetings of your group.

• You may want to design goal-setting and planning sessions for your staff that really get them involved and committed.

• You may want to develop a better plan for your annual membership meeting or work conference.

• You may want to take the great step of revolutionizing staff meetings and committee meetings to make them more productive and more exciting than they are now.

• You may want to motivate students to participate in learning activities.

Some Questions We Have Been Hearing from You

To prepare ourselves to be helpful to you, we made a list of all the questions we could remember that various ones of you have asked us over the years as we have had the challenge and fun of helping you, in many communities and types of organizations, to plan and conduct more productive, satisfying, and creative meetings. "You" are corporation presidents, agency executives, volunteer committee chairpersons, managers, program leaders, training directors, consultants, youth group leaders, teachers, etc. Here are some of the questions we have heard most frequently from you:

• "What do you have to do ahead of time to guarantee a good meeting?"

• "How do you get the members to come to the meeting?"

These are 10 dimensions which all meetings have in common, although every meeting differs from every other one on each of these dimensions. In the sections which follow we will be showing ideas and techniques to help you make the plan for each of your meetings appropriately different in relation to these dimensions of meetings.

Unit 3
Designing Participatory Meetings

$\mathbf{Y}$ou might be feeling at this point that this business of designing or planning meetings is a bit burdensome, with all the things there are to think about. Actually, this book should make the job of planning and leading a lot simpler and help prevent a wide variety of time wasting traps and errors in the leadership and planning of meetings.

Now let's turn to the actual planning of the design and flow of a session or sessions. This unit provides three guidesheets with suggestions about the process of planning, during which the meeting checklists in Unit 4 will be useful.

Several Beliefs About Planning

1. A first belief is that anyone with leadership or teaching responsibility for any type of meeting has the job of planning carefully for that event rather than "playing it by ear." Time is precious and groups need a renewal of faith that a productive experience and outcome is possible, and that an orderly, thoughtful process of involvement and collaboration can result from a good planning job.

2. A second belief is that the anticipated participant-members of the meeting or conference or workshop or class must be represented in whatever way is feasible in defining the desired outcomes of the meeting. This may be by questionnaire, or meeting with the program committee, or telephone interviews with a sample, or any other way of eliciting needs, interests, priorities, and expectations ahead of time from participants. If none of this can be done beforehand, a census of needs and expectations can be taken at the beginning of the meeting itself.

3. A third belief is that the plan for the meeting must provide the kinds of opportunities for every person to participate which will motivate their involvement and elicit and utilize their personal resources, skills and ideas.

4. Fourth, the design must make provision for getting feedback from the participants about their feelings of satisfaction, productivity or frustrations, and ideas for improvement, so that the process can be revised during the meeting and participants can experience their influence in guiding the process.

5. Follow up must be part of the planning process, including who will do what and when it will be done.

6. Feedback about participants' feedback is of the utmost importance. They must know how their input influenced the process.

Using these beliefs as a foundation, we have developed three specific planning tools and some steps for using them.

The Three Steps of Planning for a Meeting

Assuming that a decision has been made that there is reason for a meeting the first step to think of is Pre-Design Preparation. Before we can think about questions of timing and the flow of the meeting or course or conference, we must mobilize the best thinking we can about three questions. The outline for doing this is presented in Planning Sheet 1. The three questions involved in Planning Sheet 1 relate to who, what, and how:

1. Who. What can we summarize as information about the needs, interests, and expectations of the participants and the individual differences and similarities among them?

2. What. What are possible purposes/outcomes of the meeting that would actualize the needs and expectations of the participants and the planners?

3. How. What are possible activities, materials, human resources, and agenda items that would facilitate the achieving of the priority outcomes for this particular group?

In our work with planning groups we have found it particularly helpful to brainstorm on questions 2 and 3 to get out all the ideas for focusing on the questions of outcomes and ingredients and then to assign priorities. This brainstorming can be done by the planning group and/or by the planners and a few participants, or if need be at the first meeting of the group.

The second planning step is the actual design for the meeting or sequence of sessions. Planning Sheet 2 provides a format to help you with this. You will note that at the top, this page helps to summarize, from the decisions of the first planning sheet, the desired goals or outcomes which you have settled on. The rest of the page is for the plan of the startup period from the time the first participant walks through the door, and for estimating the timing and flow of the meeting, with the divisions of responsibility for leadership, the groupings, needed materials, resources, and space arrangements in the room.

The third step, Planning Sheet 3, facilitates the planning of how you want the meeting to end—announcements, commitments, followup phases, etc. and what followup activities are part of the design to insure the outcome and continuities you have as priorities. This after-the-meeting part of the design is a critical determiner of whether the time and energy of the meeting is worthwhile.

With this design for planning in mind, and the suggested planning sheets reviewed, you may want to turn to the illustrative designs of several meetings in the tool kits in Unit 8.

We would like to be able to provide each of you with the particular individualized help you need in planning your meetings, but since we can't do that we have included these sample designs as illustrations of the ways we use the three planning sheets. We recommend that you try them out.

Diagnostic Planning for Designing Participatory Meetings

WHO	WHAT	HOW
Thinking about the participants or members (e.g., how many, subgroups and individual differences, needs, readinesses, interests, expectations).	Some desirable outcomes of the meeting (e.g., skills, information, values, attitudes, concepts, actions, plans, recommendations, decisions).	Ideas for activities, experiences, resources to facilitate the outcomes (e.g., exercises, projects, resources, facilities, films, work groups).
*Star most important characteristics and differences among participants to keep in mind in designing.	*Star highest priority outcomes.	*Star what seem to be most appropriate, effective, feasible ingredients of design.

Planning Sheet No. 2

The Meeting Design: Timing, Flow, Assignments, Arrangements

Desired Outcomes or Goals:			
Time Estimate	**Activities, Methods, Groupings,**	**Who responsible**	**Arrangements of space, equipment, materials**
	(Continue on additional sheets as needed)		

Planning Sheet No. 3

Commitments, Follow-ups, Supports

1. Plans for Ending the Meeting (e.g., closing activities, evaluation, reports of back-home plans, deadline commitments, action commitments).

2. Followup Actions. Who? Will do what? When? Where? (e.g., often a directory of names, addresses, telephone numbers of participants is very important at this point, and getting any followup dates recorded in everyone's calendar).

3. Cleanup and Other Immediate Commitments (e.g., what has to be returned, thank-you calls made, bills paid, furniture put back in original order).

Unit 4
Checklists for Planning Meetings

I︎t is so easy to forget some crucial items in the planning of meetings—some materials you wanted to be sure to have available, the telephone call to the custodian, the name tags, extra minutes of the last meeting, and many others. We have found it indispensable, and very embarrassment-preventing to have a checklist to review and check off as part of the process of planning and leading meetings. The ones on the following pages should be a good starter; one can add to them because all meetings, of course, are different—all items are not relevant for every meeting. But in our experience the main headings and most of the items are quite universal.

The checklists are organized under:

1. Publicity, Promotion, Notifying
2. Agenda and Resource Materials
3. Responsibilities at the Meeting
4. Space Check-out
5. Equipment for the Meeting
6. Materials for the Meeting
7. Budget
8. Just before the Meeting
9. At the Meeting
10. After the Meeting

The checklists on the following pages complement our three planning sheets in Unit 3 and the tool kits in Unit 8.

1. PUBLICITY/PROMOTION/NOTIFYING

		Who Responsible	By When
_____	notices—to whom	_____	_____
_____	letters of invitation	_____	_____
_____	directions to meeting place	_____	_____
_____	phone calls	_____	_____
_____	news releases	_____	_____
_____	contact with the media	_____	_____
_____	copies of speeches	_____	_____
_____	copies of meeting plan	_____	_____
_____	pictures/photographs	_____	_____
_____	bulletin boards	_____	_____
_____	personal contacts	_____	_____
_____	other	_____	_____
_____		_____	_____
_____		_____	_____
_____		_____	_____

2. AGENDA AND RESOURCE MATERIALS

	Who Responsible	By When
_____ copies of agenda	_____	_____
_____ contact people on the agenda	_____	_____
_____ materials needed (e.g., reprints)	_____	_____
_____ previous minutes	_____	_____
_____ committee reports	_____	_____
_____ previous agreements and time commitments	_____	_____
_____ other	_____	_____
_____	_____	_____
_____	_____	_____
_____	_____	_____

3. RESPONSIBILITIES BEFORE THE MEETING   Who Responsible   By When

	Who Responsible	By When
_____ leadership assignments	_____	_____
_____ documentation or recording assignments	_____	_____
_____ resource persons?	_____	_____
_____ observers?	_____	_____
_____ "hosting" roles	_____	_____
_____ making reports	_____	_____
_____ trying out all equipment	_____	_____
_____ test whether charts, posters are readable	_____	_____
_____ test electrical outlets	_____	_____
_____ preview films for timing & content	_____	_____
_____ other	_____	_____
_____	_____	_____
_____	_____	_____
_____	_____	_____

4. SPACE CHECK OUT

		Who Responsible	By When
_____ size and shape of space		_____	_____
_____ electrical outlets		_____	_____
_____ mike outlets		_____	_____
_____ acoustics		_____	_____
_____ doors		_____	_____
_____ bathrooms (where, no. can accommodate)		_____	_____
_____ stairs		_____	_____
_____ elevators		_____	_____
_____ heat/cold regulation		_____	_____
_____ ventilation		_____	_____
_____ parking facilities: cost, number, & access		_____	_____
_____ registration area		_____	_____
_____ location		_____	_____
_____ transportation, access to facility		_____	_____
_____ room setup arrangements		_____	_____
_____ access to meeting room(s)		_____	_____
_____ lighting		_____	_____
_____ name of custodian/engineering, where to be reached		_____	_____
_____ telephone access for messages and calling out		_____	_____
_____ exhibit space		_____	_____
_____ wall space for newsprints, etc.		_____	_____
_____ emotional impact (color, aesthetics)		_____	_____
_____ room-darkening possibilities		_____	_____
_____ areas for disabled		_____	_____
_____ other		_____	_____
_____		_____	_____
_____		_____	_____

5. EQUIPMENT FOR MEETING

	Who Responsible	By When
_____ tables (number, size, shape)	_____	_____
_____ chairs (comfort, number)	_____	_____
_____ microphones	_____	_____
_____ audio tape recorder	_____	_____
_____ audio tape cassettes	_____	_____
_____ video tape recorder	_____	_____
_____ video tape cassettes	_____	_____
_____ extension cords	_____	_____
_____ overhead projector	_____	_____
_____ newsprint easel (chart stand)	_____	_____
_____ film projector	_____	_____
_____ chalkboard-chalk	_____	_____
_____ chalkboard eraser	_____	_____
_____ typewriters	_____	_____
_____ waste baskets	_____	_____
_____ bulletin boards	_____	_____
_____ pillows	_____	_____
_____ projection table(s)	_____	_____
_____ flannel board	_____	_____
_____ easel	_____	_____
_____ slide projector	_____	_____
_____ screen	_____	_____
_____ platform	_____	_____
_____ record/disc/tape player	_____	_____
_____ records, discs, tapes	_____	_____
_____ gavel	_____	_____
_____ coffee, tea dispensers	_____	_____
_____ water pitchers	_____	_____
_____ cups	_____	_____
_____ camera	_____	_____
_____ film	_____	_____
_____ transparencies & appropriate pens & grease pencils	_____	_____
_____ extension cords	_____	_____
_____ duplication equipment	_____	_____

6. MATERIALS AND SUPPLIES FOR THE MEETING

	Who Responsible	By When
_____ name tags/tents	_____	_____
_____ small tip felt pens	_____	_____
_____ large tip felt pens	_____	_____
_____ masking tape	_____	_____
_____ paper clips	_____	_____
_____ crayons	_____	_____
_____ pins	_____	_____
_____ scissors	_____	_____
_____ stapler	_____	_____
_____ glue	_____	_____
_____ newsprint paper	_____	_____
_____ scratch paper	_____	_____
_____ pencils	_____	_____
_____ duplication supplies	_____	_____
_____ self carbon paper	_____	_____
_____ reprints of articles	_____	_____
_____ copies of previous minutes	_____	_____
_____ copies of reports	_____	_____
_____ books	_____	_____
_____ visual aids	_____	_____
_____ puppets	_____	_____
_____ colored paper	_____	_____
_____ pamphlets	_____	_____
_____ display materials	_____	_____
_____ flowers or flower arrangements	_____	_____
_____ decorations	_____	_____
_____ posters	_____	_____
_____ instruction sheets	_____	_____
_____ resume of resource people	_____	_____
_____ directional signs (to meeting)	_____	_____
_____ chalk (various colors)	_____	_____
_____ file folders	_____	_____
_____ other	_____	_____
_____	_____	_____

7. BUDGET*

Costs   **Estimated Cost**

_____ mailing and stamps   _____

_____ telephone calls   _____

_____ telephone conferences   _____

_____ rental of equipment   _____

_____ rental of space   _____

_____ paper materials   _____

   _____ name tags   _____

   _____ newsprint   _____

   _____ paper   _____

   _____ construction   paper   _____

_____ writing materials   _____

   _____ pens   _____

   _____ crayons   _____

   _____ special pens for overhead   _____

   _____ grease pencils   _____

_____ secretarial/computer time   _____

_____ transportation   _____

_____ meals   _____

_____ bar   _____

_____ coffee, tea, juice   _____

_____ reproduction of materials   _____

_____ folders   _____

_____ tapes   _____

_____ operator of multimedia equipment   _____

_____ operator of P.A. equipment   _____

_____ speaker fees   _____

_____ consultant fees   _____

_____ entertainment   _____

_____ flowers   _____

_____ film reproduction   _____

_____ tape reproduction   _____

_____ other   _____

_____

*Some of these will not be budget cost items for some planners.

Income   **Estimated Income**

_____ registration fees   _____

_____ sale of materials   _____

_____ grants   _____

_____ sale of meal tickets   _____

_____ donations   _____

_____ membership fees   _____

_____ coffee and tea charges   _____

_____ in-kind bartering   _____

_____ other   _____

_____   _____

_____   _____

_____   _____

8. JUST BEFORE THE MEETING

_____ seating arrangements—general session and subgroupings	_____
_____ extra chairs	_____
_____ extra tables	_____
_____ P.A. system checkout	_____
_____ equipment (easels, screens, etc.)	_____
_____ materials (paper, pens, etc.)	_____
_____ water, glasses	_____
_____ thermostat	_____
_____ opening and closing of windows	_____
_____ refreshment setup	_____
_____ registration setup	_____
_____ check that charts, boards, screens can be seen from everywhere	_____
_____ agendas available	_____
_____ other materials available for handouts	_____
_____ name tags/tents	_____
_____ table numbers	_____
_____ coffee, tea, etc.	_____
_____ evaluation forms ready	_____
_____ reproduction equipment	_____
_____ audio-visual equipment ready	_____
_____ other	_____
_____	_____
_____	_____
_____	_____

9. AT THE MEETING

_____ meeting, greeting, seating of participants   _____
                        and guests

_____ documentation—recording   _____

_____ greeting of latecomers   _____

_____ evaluation activities   _____

_____ handing out materials   _____

_____ operation of equipment   _____

_____ process review, stop sessions, etc.   _____

_____ announcements   _____

_____ other   _____

_____   _____

_____   _____

_____   _____

10. END OF MEETING—AND AFTER　　　　　　　　　　　　　　　**Who Responsible**　　**By When**

_____ collect unused materials　　　　　　_____　　_____

_____ return equipment　　　　　　　　　　_____　　_____

_____ clean up　　　　　　　　　　　　　　_____　　_____

_____ thank helpers　　　　　　　　　　　　_____　　_____

_____ read and analyze evaluation/feedback　_____　　_____

_____ prepare feedback on feedback　　　　_____　　_____

_____ mail follow-up materials　　　　　　　_____　　_____

_____ remind people of their follow-up
　　　　　　　　　　commitments—phone _____

　　　　　　　　　　　　　　write _____

_____ lay plans for next meeting; dates if　　_____　　_____
　　　　　　　　　　there is to be one

_____ pay bills　　　　　　　　　　　　　　_____　　_____

_____ collect outstanding monies　　　　　_____　　_____

_____ follow-up phone calls　　　　　　　　_____　　_____

_____ reports　　　　　　　　　　　　　　_____　　_____

_____ other　　　　　　　　　　　　　　　_____　　_____

_____　　　　　　　　　　　　　　　　　_____　　_____

_____　　　　　　　　　　　　　　　　　_____　　_____

_____　　　　　　　　　　　　　　　　　_____　　_____

A few ideas about the use of these checklists:

For your particular kinds of meetings or classes you may want to create an abbreviated checklist. We suggest you reproduce whatever form is appropriate for you, making enough copies so that you and your co-workers can use one for each planning activity.

　　Then you will also have it available to hand to other associates to whom you care to give help and support in their planning and leading of meetings.

　　In the next unit there is another kind of checklist of program resources you may find helpful to scan as you plan the content of your meetings.

Unit 5
Resources for Program Planning

In addition to the ingredients needed for a successful meeting, there are all kinds of resources that will enrich your program planning and implementation. Here we are describing some human and experience resources, written resources and some of the possible purposes for including them, or special ways to tap them to enrich the program of the meeting.

Also there are some tips and traps about utilizing people, experiences and the written word.

Resources (People) Checklist

Resource	Purpose
1. Participants, Members	• to help plan as subgroup leaders • to give ideas • to make decisions
2. Speakers	• to bring information as triggers for discussion • to answer questions
3. "Expert Consultants"	• to teach special skills • to lead participative meetings • to moderate a meeting or panel
4. Leader(s)	• to convene • to facilitate activities • to utilize other people
5. Secretary	• to document what goes on • to teach others how to record
6. Librarian	• to organize relevant materials • to check materials in and out • to develop a display of written materials
7. Custodian	• to help with room setup • to gather necessary equipment

Tips and Traps
in Utilizing Human Resources

Tips

1. Let people know before the meeting if you are going to ask them to do something (e.g., record, lead a subgroup, etc.).
   - Agree on the task
   - Agree on the time & timing
   - Orient them to meeting participants and to the program
2. For member participation give clear instructions—preferably written and verbal.
3. Meet with outside speakers and consultants ahead of time, if possible.
   - If not, have a telephone conference with them.
   - And/or write a memo describing your request and ask for an answer in writing.
4. Ask your helpers (e.g., secretary, custodian, librarian) several days ahead rather than at the last minute.

Traps

1. No set time limits:
   - for speakers
   - for agenda items
   - for participation by group members
2. No clear contract with persons as to what is expected of them and what they expect of you.
3. No clear communication of the purpose of the meeting.
4. No recognition of the participation and contribution of others.
5. Assuming they'll know "what's needed" and "what's expected" without a personal briefing session.

Resources (Direct Experiences) Checklist

Resource	Purpose
1. Role Playing and Behavioral Skill Practice	• to practice new skills (e.g., handling hostility or making a speech) • to learn how to empathize • to do anticipatory practice (e.g., telling your boss you want a raise before you actually do it)
2. Simulations	• to learn through trying out and participating in an (artificial) situation that is patterned after real life situations—e.g., power struggles, inter-agency collaboration, voter education
3. Field Trips, Direct Observations	• to observe experience and see relevant sites, experiences, exhibits, etc. (e.g., how an alternate school really functions—how different people live & worship.)
4. Small-group decision making, problem solving	• to learn the pros and cons before making a decision • to get a feeling for the complexity of problems to be solved • to help people "own" the decisions they are making and which affect them
5. Video Taping	• to practice a skill (e.g., how to interview and learn to analyze your own verbal and non-verbal behavior) • to document proceedings of a group • to give feedback to a small group
6. Audio Taping	• to record a speech • to record a part of a meeting for purpose of analysis • to record a short critical confrontation situation for purposes of playing it to a group for discussion and developing alternative solutions
7. Brainstorms	• to get many ideas out in a short time, maximizing participants' resources

Tips and Traps
About Providing Direct Experiences

Tips

1. Learning through experiencing is one of the best ways to acquire new or additional skills, ideas, understandings.
2. When helping people learn new skills give them opportunities to practice and repractice until they feel they have acquired the skill they are practicing.
3. Be sure the role playing situations (see tool kit in Unit 8) and simulations are as near to real life as is possible.
4. The anticipation planning session ahead of time and the review of learnings afterward are critical phases of a field trip.
5. In any audio or video recording, test and re-test whether equipment is working, sound is loud enough, recording conditions of room are O.K., etc.

Traps

1. No observation plans for field trips
2. Untested equipment
3. Too little equipment for the number of participants
4. No time for de-briefing after role playing and/or simulations
5. Lack of "division of responsibility"—plans for the activity
6. Making the recordings too long so playbacks are boring and too time consuming

Resources (Written Materials) Checklist

Resource	Purpose
1. Displays of pamphlets & books	• to acquaint participants with additional resources • to check out and read (at least in part) as part of the meeting design • to read & critique
2. Articles—published and unpublished	• for critiques • to provide up-to-date information as background reading
3. Multi-media resources (e.g., a book with audio/video tapes/discs)	• for group discussion • for information • for problem solving
4. Instructions	• so groups can start without verbal instructions • to clarify verbal instructions
5. Background papers	• to give information needed • to make meetings useful • as discussion trigger
6. Poetry & other readings, quotes	• to set atmosphere • to illustrate a point • to summarize

Tips and Traps
in Relation to the Use
of Written Materials

Tips

1. If you want materials read be sure to give time during all meetings for it.
2. Have enough copies of written materials available.
3. Written instructions can be on the overhead projector or on newsprint sheets around the room or individual copies on the tables.
4. Test instructions ahead of time to see if they are clear to participants of the meeting. They may need to be in several languages.
5. If using multimedia (e.g., audio tapes) check beforehand to make sure they work and are set up.
6. Displays and exhibits are most useful if people are with them to explain them and answer questions.

Traps

1. To send materials ahead of time and assume everyone will read them.
2. Material that is too lengthy.
3. Quoting without adequate identification of the source.
4. Articles and/or books filled with technical jargon.
5. Articles, chapters, or parts of books that are too long for easy reading.
6. Making no use in the meeting of reading that has been done.

This is a reminder checklist to scan and add to as you use it in your own planning activities, or help others to do their planning of meetings. The tool kit provides you with additional suggestions about the procedures for using these resources.

Unit 6
Some Traps in Planning
and Conducting Meetings

One of the greatest resources for all of us is the ability to learn from our achievements. Another good resource is the opportunity to learn from our mistakes, and from the learnings of others who have "tried that before" and have been innovative in finding ways to avoid traps and improve upon their successes.

The planning and conducting of thousands of meetings has preceded the ones you are planning this year. To avoid even a few of the mistakes and to learn from some of the many creative inventions will greatly increase your skills and successes.

In this chapter is some of the knowledge pooled from our own mistakes and discoveries along with that of many others from whom we have learned.

Here are a few of the most critical traps to the planning and leading of successful meetings. No doubt you can add to these right now from your experience, and hopefully will be able to identify, analyze, and share additional traps during the next year—and share them with other colleagues.

Let's list traps during the planning of a meeting, and during the conducting of a meeting.

Traps During Planning and Preparation

1. Planning with no data. Meeting planners often plan with no data about the participants, their hopes and expectations about the purpose of the meeting. Often meetings are planned in a vacuum with no idea about who is coming, why they are coming, or really what specifically ought to be accomplished at the meeting. It is critical to go through the kind of cycle that has been suggested earlier (see Unit 4) and, if one does not have the needed information, to discover ways of getting it.

2. Lack of involvement in the planning by those who will be at the meeting. When potential participants are not involved in some way they'll probably not take an active part, or they may not even come. They feel they have been planned for, so their attitude is: let the planners do it! We have no "ownership" of this meeting!

3. ***Beautiful, but illegible, visual aids.*** So often visual aids are produced that are visually very pleasing but have not been tried out in large rooms or have not been tested for the distance from which they can be seen. Be sure to check all your visual aids beforehand, and all pieces of equipment, in the room where they are to be used.

4. ***Same meeting, same place and plan, same time.*** Though sameness gives security to some, it bores others. Why not vary the meeting, place and time to suit different people of the group? Or ask group members what, where, when they'd like to meet next time. If the meeting extends for a whole day or longer, and participants keep going back to the same seats, suggest they change.

5. ***Holding meetings only because they are scheduled to be held.*** If there is no real reason or agenda for a meeting, why hold it? Yes, even if it is a planned monthly meeting. Can you imagine how motivated members would feel for the next meeting if they could count on its being really meaty and full of content, knowing that if there would be nothing to discuss you'd cancel it?

6. ***Equipment that does not work.*** Check your equipment beforehand, but even when equipment checks out it sometimes breaks down at the time you most need it. So have an alternative plan up your sleeve, just in case.

7. ***Lack of plans if extra people turn up.*** Often meetings that are projected for 50 people have 75 to 100 people come. It is important to have some contingency plans. In case that happens, i.e., is there a way to move or walk to a larger room? Are there extra tables and chairs available? What if the opposite happens, and fewer people than were planned for show up? Can the room be made cozy and useful in some way, rather than have people feel as though they are rattling around in a large empty room?

8. ***The unbriefed resource person or speaker.*** A speaker may have no idea about what you really wanted and what the group is like and will give the usual canned speech that is always given on that particular topic by that particular person. It is extremely important to brief people beforehand whom you want as resource persons for your meeting. These briefings can be done over the telephone, by letter or in person, depending on the situation. Sometimes the resource person will send an outline of what she/he will cover.

9. ***No agenda or inadequate agenda.*** For some meetings no agenda exists or if it does it is only in the head and maybe the hand of the leader. Also it is important to review and communicate the purpose(s) of each meeting.

10. ***Too many items/activities for the time available.*** This is a trap that many meetings fall into, and a realistic plan is needed in relation to how much time various items or activities will take. If you have more items than the time allows then cut out some items, or else arrange to put them in as pieces you can work on in small groups after the meeting or substitute these for items of lower priorities.

Traps During the Meeting

11. ***No sharing of agenda.*** There is only one copy of the agenda available, and the chairperson has that. It is hard for participants/members to feel involved when they cannot see and hear the plans of the meeting.

12. *Formal, classroom style seating* (i.e., rows of chairs all facing the front). This gives the participants the non-verbal clue that all action and wisdom comes from the front of the room. It makes it hard to participate actively. The only reason to have this kind of room setup is when the seats are fastened to the floor. Then participants must be helped to participate in special ways, such as two turning around to the two behind them to talk, or a stand-up break of trios or quintets to discuss a particular question. So long as there are movable chairs they can be in a circle or small semi-circle or around tables, or other ways that invite and facilitate communication.

13. *Meeting starts with nothing to do for early arrivers.* If you know that your meeting will have a "raggedy start," plan something for the ahead timers to do, discuss, or think about. It may be a question you want them to discuss, or it may be the use of the paired interview, or it may be some other way to get together in a table group. There needs to be some pro- grammed way to utilize the pre-starting time constructively.

14. *Long introductions.* Long introductions of speakers, consultants, and helpers usually produce psychological distance between them and the participants. If you need an extensive introduction/background material on a person in order to acquaint them with that person, have those materials reproduced for everyone beforehand. Or give them out at the beginning of the meeting. Then you can give a short, warm, relevant welcome instead of a long introduc- tion. Often the speakers have ideas how they would like to be introduced.

15. *Long, drawn-out speeches and reports.* Often people go over the time limits they have been given. It is important to go over the ground rules with them at the beginning of the meeting again, after having done so in preparing them to participate. And often it is well to reinforce this publicly by saying to all present: "the time of the following presentation is approximately 12 minutes," or: "I have discussed with our resource person the amount of time available, so don't worry if I give a warning when the time is almost up." Or put a large watch in sight of the speaker.

16. *Total reliance on one expert.* The expert should be utilized to help uncork the resources of all the participants. Sometimes it is better to have more than one resource person available, so that alternatives can be more openly and fully identified.

17. *Long coffee breaks.* A long coffee break can waste time and money and also disrupt the continuity. Why not have coffee and tea available throughout the meeting and design the meeting in such a way that there will be moving around and stand-up time as part of the way the work of the meeting gets done?

18. *Failure to deal with feelings of participants.* Often groups are so task-oriented, that they skip even obvious feeling issues that need to be dealt with in order to better proceed with the task. For example, if people are very hostile to one another, it is important to deal with that hostility rather than overlook it. The task will get done much better if this is done. (See Stop Sessions in Tool Kit B.)

19. *No record of what has been said or done.* Often, when you most want to go back to what happened at a meeting, there is no record of the proceedings. It is important that for every meeting there is some way to keep its major deliberations and work in a documented form. This can then become the history of that meeting, and of plans, decisions, commit- ments made.

20. *Neglecting to carry the group "into the future."* To guarantee that the work of the meeting will pay off, it is important to be sure that decisions and commitments are made about *who* will do *what* and *when* to follow through.

Undoubtedly you can add some additional traps from your experiences with meetings. We hope this list will be helpful in ensuring better meetings for you, your participants, and your programs.

Unit 7
Some Things that Come up in Meetings:
Ideas on What To Do

There are some things that occur again and again during meetings. Here are some examples of typical events and episodes. We have suggested some ideas on how to handle these situations. We hope you will add your own alternative solutions. Here are eight typical confronting situations:

1. Cutting a long-winded speaker
2. Coping with latecomers
3. Coping with high-status person
4. Stimulating a non-reactive, passive group
5. Coping with different time norms
6. Dealing with long committee reports
7. Dealing with experts
8. Physical setups

Question 1. Long-Winded Speaker

How would you cut a long-winded speaker?

Alternative Ideas:

1. One of the things one can do is confer briefly ahead of time with the suggestion to make one or two stops in the speech in order to give listeners a chance to ask questions or make comments.
2. Another one is to advise the speaker beforehand that you will give a time warning so many minutes before the end.
3. Sometimes you can stand up at a given time.

4. Or you can sit next to the speaker so you can give a "touch signal."

5. Another one is to have a timekeeper in the audience, previously agreed upon, who stands up at an agreed-upon time.

6. One of the most important ways is to make very clear to the speaker ahead of time about how long a speech the group is expecting.

7. Another way is to say to the whole group something like: "Dr. So and So will speak approximately 20 minutes, after which you'll be able to ask questions."

Question 2. Latecomers

One of the problems is the puzzling issue of latecomers after things have gotten underway. What can you do?

Alternative Ideas:

1. One of the things you could do would be to have one or several people designated to greet and update the late people.

2. Perhaps have a separate table near the door so people can pick up any needed material as they come in.

3. Another one, if you have a number of tables, is to leave one or two spaces open at each table and have someone ready to invite the latecomers to join already formed groups.

4. It is effective to have established a pattern of always starting on time. Then people know that if they are late, they will miss something.

5. It is important to include the latecomers as quickly as possible, since they may feel guilty about being late.

Question 3. VIPs

The national president of the organization is going to be at the next meeting. What are some of the ways to make the group feel at ease with this person in attendance?

Alternative Ideas:

1. Have a coffee hour at the beginning of the meeting where people can meet the person informally.

2. Utilize the VIP early in the meeting so there is no necessity for anxiety or prolonged curiosity.

3. Have different seating arrangements so the national president is not always at the head table. The president might sit at different tables in the room with different people, to get to know some of them.

4. Or perhaps the president could eat beforehand and then walk around and meet people during the course of the meal.

5. Or the president could have a different course at different tables.

6. Or give the president a place on the agenda to ask questions of the group so that he/she can demonstrate an interest and a posture of inquiry toward the group itself.

7. Ask the president what he/she would like to do to get in touch with the group.

Question 4. Unresponsive Group

You've heard chairpeople say: "Gosh, what do I do with that group? You ask them a question and they just don't respond; they're apathetic; I just don't know where they are."

Alternative Ideas:

1. One way to handle it might be to break down into buzz groups or table groups to discuss the issue at hand, and then have a rotating report back to the total group.

2. Another thing is to ask for a brainstorm in which you do away with the pressure of evaluation of discussion by having everybody stimulate each other by calling out ideas.

3. Another one might be to divide them into trios and have them come up with all the ways "we could get our group to participate more."

4. You could have a guided discussion sheet about the topic available for each table.

5. Or, you might train some conveners for small groups so that the convener can help that group participate more actively.

6. Challenge them by asking them, "What questions would you ask a group about this?"

Question 5. Starting Time

One roadblock for many meetings is the issue of starting a meeting at a particular time: Do you start at the stated time or when people arrive?

Alternative Ideas:

1. One approach is to recognize that even in the best of groups people aren't going to walk in the door at the same time, and therefore it is best to have plans for what you might call a "ragged beginning" in which there is something to do from the moment the first member comes in; for example, suggestions for some pre-meeting conversation topics or some things to skim and read or some short interviews of each other.

2. Or you can establish the pattern of starting on time and then catching up the latecomers later.

3. Another idea is to do some small-group tasks as people come in to the meeting. The total group portion of the meeting doesn't start until the small groups are all ready to report out to the whole group.

4. Another thing that works sometimes is to get away from the assumption that the leadership has the responsibility for taking the rap of being disciplinary or calling attention to people who are late. Instead, have a committee of peers that works on an approach to late members and then calls attention of the group to its own norms. So, it's a member of the group rather than the leader who has the job of dealing with the problem.

5. Another way is to have the whole group discuss "what we might do about some people coming early and some people coming late, and how we as a group might handle it."

6. Or, you might test the starting time for this group. Is it realistic, or was it set by a small number of people for their convenience? Or, was it set many years ago and has never been challenged?

Question 6. Reports

One of the things that we face as a kind of puzzle in most groups is how to deal with committee reports, including the reading of lengthy minutes of previous meetings. How can you deal with this?

Alternative Ideas:

1. One thing is to require a time limit, so that you may not have more than two minutes to report out, and then to cut off the report.

2. Or it could be a requirement that the committees have summary reports at each member's place so there can be a reading period, and then instead of a report out there is a responding to questions on the part of those who have just finished reading it.

3. Or, another one is to ask work groups to hand in their written report for the sake of the record, but report verbally only the three most exciting things that happened, or the two things about which they want responses from the other group members.

4. You might have someone interview the chairperson of the committee to distinctly spell out highlights: a kind of public interview.

5. Another way is to have the report in the form of a mobile design, large drawing, or even ask groups to act it out non-verbally, rather than thinking of it as only in written or spoken form.

Question 7. Inviting and Briefing Experts

Often we invite expert resource people. How do we decide who we want, and then how do we brief that person to make sure he/she is really useful?

Alternative Ideas:

1. Sometimes give or send the expert a summary of actions, problems, or situations that the group has experienced relating to the resource person's specialty.

2. Sometimes it's possible to have a brief brainstorm or listing at previous meetings around some of the things the members of the group hope to learn or get clarified or solved in the session with the resource person.

3. You could have a panel discussion at the beginning of the meeting with questions from a few members and answers from the resource person.

4. You could have either a personal or telephone conference among two or three members of the group and the resource person.

5. Ahead of time, advise the resource person that the group has some definite ideas they want to explore, and that they are preparing those in order to save the speaker the trouble of preparing a speech. They want to use him/her as a resource responder rather than as a speaker.

6. Be very clear with the resource person in regard to the length of time, the topic and the hoped-for outcomes of the meeting.

7. Ask the resource person how he/she would like to handle the situation. Also ask if there are special ideas he/she wants to share.

Question 8. Meeting-Room Setups

I've just walked in the door of the room where we're going to hold our meeting and the setup is nothing like I asked for. What now?

Alternative Ideas:

1. Well, you have several choices; one is to get busy and rearrange it.

2. Rearrange either by yourself or by getting several others to help you move the tables out of those fixed, straight-line patterns or move the chairs away from the classic rows, etc.

3. Sometimes you can find out where the custodian is, and ask him/her to please help you rearrange it.

4. Or have this be part of the start-up as people come in and make it a fun kind of work session with their help.

5. It is important to have clear plans for the kind of groupings that are needed for the meeting activity so that you can look at the space and say: "We're going to start our meeting with circles of five, or we want semi-circles of six that can close up and make circles later on in the program."

6. Hopefully you've been there beforehand and have done some careful planning as to how to use this space, so that you know what you're going to do now.

7. You could also scout the building to see if there is an empty room that would be easier to set up in a quicker manner.

8. Also, there is frequently a very formal kind of rostrum or platform in the front, and it may be important to try and destroy the authority image of "the speaker from the pulpit" by changing the concept of where the front of the room is and what is going to happen from there.

Now that you have reviewed our ideas about these critical kinds of questions, you might want to take each one and reflect on what additional ideas you have for handling them. Certainly there are many more possibilities. These are just a beginning to help get you triggered to add some of your own solutions.

This kind of rehearsal to develop your repertoire of solutions will do much to enhance your creativity when such situations occur. We recommend you try this same type of brainstorming alternatives about other critical issues of meeting leadership.

Unit 8
Ideas and Resources
To Help with Your Meetings

This unit provides six tool kits to help with your meetings. The contents of these tool kits are as follows:

Tool Kit A: Illustrative Designs and Plans

1. Sample Meeting Designs and Plans
   - a one-day retreat
   - regular monthly board meeting
   - community theater program committee
   - music-center volunteer meeting
   - symposium in community leadership
   - how to teach: facilitating learning
   - better meetings for large corporate systems
2. Sample Physical Arrangements Briefing Sheet
   - sample diagrams
3. Sample Agenda Sheet

Tool Kit B: Beginnings of Meetings

1. Greeting Sheet
2. Paired Interview
3. Name Tags
4. Sign-In Sheet
5. Individual Identification Sheets

Tool Kit C: Looking at Process and Participation

1. "Stop Session"
2. How are we Doing?
3. Outside Consultant
4. End of Meeting Feedback
5. Some Samples

Tool Kit D: Getting Ideas Out and Shared

1. Brainstorming
2. Small-Group Techniques
   - buzz groups
   - small work groups
3. Samples of Self-Inquiry and Evaluation Methods
4. Sharing and Integrating Ideas
5. Exchange of Successful Practices
6. From Goals to Action: Participative Planning
7. Ideas for Effective Work Teams
8. Parliamentary Know-How
9. Most-Used Motions

Tool Kit E: Goal Setting and Action Planning

1. Eight Sources of Goals
2. Discovering and Choosing Goals by Images of Potentiality
3. A Sequence of Action Planning

Tool Kit F: Role Playing and Skill Practice

1. Skill Practice Episodes
2. Using Role-Playing Methods

These are condensed illustrations of the use of the planning procedures and sheets discussed in Unit 3. A sample physical arrangement sheet is included, as well as an illustrative meeting agenda plan. These are just springboards for your own adaptations, and resource ideas to share as you help others develop their skills of planning meetings.

TOOL KIT A: ILLUSTRATIVE DESIGNS AND PLANS

A One-Day Retreat, 9 A.M.—5 P.M.

20 staff members to plan a staff training program for the year

Preplanning Sheet		
Participating Members (Who)	**Desirable Outcomes (What)**	**Ideas for activities, exper., resources, facilities (How)**
• 20 staff members representing a total staff of 60 • They are the profess. dev. comm. of the agency • Represent various depts. • Men & women ages 25-57 • Are eager to plan a good program • Some had been in the agency 15 years, others from 1 yr. on • Staff dev. seen as an important benefit of working in this agency as it's good in-service training	*1. That all planning staff get to know each other as human beings 2. They get to know and understand each other's jobs 3. They thoroughly analyze staff needs & requests 4. They discover an area or areas of emphasis for staff development *5. They develop a preliminary design for the year's training plan 6. They develop a strategy of how to share their design with the rest of the staff & get feedback	A good accessible facility Arr. for meals Newsprint Duplicating equipment and supplies, pens, masking tape Various groupings Welcome warmup Staff questionnaires Design outline Anticipatory role playing Outside consultant Brainstorming

Summary of Outcomes: The planning group becomes a group and develops a staff development plan for the year.

*Most important to keep in mind	*Highest priority

Planning Sheet			
Time	**Activities and Methods**	**Who resp.**	**Arrangements, etc.**
8:30	The Beginning • Directional signs to meeting in place • Check on room & coffee-tea setup • Open windows & door • Have name tags ready • Greet people as they come in • Music on	2 comm. members	Chairs arranged for pairs to interview each other. Newsprint File folders String Pens—large, small Masking tape Name tags Tape recorders Audio cassettes Music records, tapes, discs, and equipment to play Ext. cord Duplicating machines and supplies
9:00	• Ask persons to interview someone they don't know well and put the info on a file folder with their name on it. 1. Name 2. What they most enjoy in life. 3. What they enjoy most about their jobs. 4. What their own training needs are		
9:30	They wander around with their own file folders around their necks and meet the others, reading & discussing each other's.		Music on in background
9:30-9:40	Quick total group discussion of interesting discoveries they made about each other.	Chair-person	
9:45	In 5 groups of 4 they read approx. 15 of the answered staff questionnaires re staff dev. needs, make a summary for duplication.	Head of questionnaire task force	 Seating arrangements
10:30	Duplicated materials are handed out & shared and major needs pulled out by total group & recorded on newsprint.	and a volunteer from the group	Newsprint
11:00	Discussion of the major needs in total group. Nomination of "candidates" to be tackled this year.	Chair-person	Newsprint
11:30	All "candidates" are listed on newsprint & each person is asked to vote for 2 priorities by putting check on the newsprint.		Large felt-tip pens
11:40-11:50	Decision made & group divides itself into 3 task forces by choice.	Chair	

Time	Activities and Methods	Who resp.	Arrangement, Etc.
12 noon	Lunch No official program Time to talk, get more acquainted Consultant joins them & is introduced		—at small tables —served in next room
1:10	Presentation with discussion of how to design meetings & programs	Consul-tant now does con-sultation with each group	Design forms
1:30 3:00	Divide into 3 task forces to design training topics 1. Consulting skills 2. Training skills 3. Organization of time Three groups use consultant's design forms outlining how to design—to do their own plan of prof. devel. in their topic area on newsprint.		Newsprint Pens Tape
3:05	3 designs are put on the wall for the other 2 groups to look at, critique & understand. Consultant helps, too.	Consultant	
3:45	Some comments by consultant on the designs & ideas for implemen-tation.	Consultant	
4:00	Total group brainstorms all the ways to communicate their plans & designs to the rest of the staff	Ch.person & one group member	Brainstorm rules on newsprint
4:15	They select priority ways to do this		
4:30	End of the Meeting Total group discussion of who will do what to implement their chosen ideas. Group call out about feelings about the day. Everyone gets a copy of agreed-upon action plans & tentative dates. They set date, time and place for a follow-up meeting to report to each other.	Chair	Record
5:00	Linger longer—some stay to have drinks with one another & to talk		

Follow-up Actions:
• Make arrangements
   1. for reproduction of designs
   2. for feedback of questionnaire results
• Thank you and payment to consultant
• Preparation of memo to all staff re: plans and preliminary dates
• Notice for next planning committee meeting

Regular Monthly Board Meeting, noon to 2 p.m.

30 persons

Preplanning Sheet		
Participants/members —their char. & needs	**Desirable outcomes of this meeting**	**Ideas for activities, experiences, resources, facilities**
• 25 males ages 24-60 • 5 females ages 35-55 • 20 members or experienced Bd. members • 10 are new this year • Mixed racial picture, native Amer., white and black, Asian • *Some of the older members are on deck. They think it's a good thing to do. • *Some of the younger members want to help change the organization to become more relevant.	1. Mixing of old and new so they get to know each other better. 2. Discussion and decision on the affirmative action program. *3. Increased understanding of the agency's budget needs and budget situation. *4. A feeling of commitment and cohesion. 5. Discussion of nominating committee report with time to add ideas. 6. Recruiting members to work on the future planning committee.	Sitting in pre-arranged mixed groups of 5 Brief reading material on affirmative action requirements Small-group discussion before vote Overhead transparencies with pictures of situation (overhead projector) Lunch of ½ hr.—sandwiches & Cokes, coffee, tea, with discussion on how we could improve our board meetings Report of these discussions to total board
Summary of Desired Outcomes: To do some specific business and to increase board cohesion.		
*Most important to keep in mind	*Highest priority	

Planning Sheet			
Time	**Activity and Methods**	**Who resp. for what**	**Arrangements & Resources room, mat., equipment**
11:30	Beginning of Meeting • Check on room arrangement • Check on luncheon & drink setup and availability • Make sure mat. & equipment are there and working • Have name tents ready for people to put their names on • Have seating chart up so people can find their table numbered 1 to 5 (assigned for mixed seating, new & old, young & older, male & female, etc.) • Meet early and on-time comers personally • Directional signs to meeting place	Leader and two greeters	6 tables (round) for 5 persons, chairs, paper and pencils, name tents, agendas Sandwiches & beverages, paper plates, napkins, cups, salt & pepper, cream & sugar Newsprint Overhead proj. Overhead transpar. Overhead pens Seating chart Nos. on tables Instruments for lunch convenient on each table
12:00 noon	• As people come in they pick up their sandwich and beverage • A colored card on each table suggests that members discuss how bd. meetings could be improved and the greeters help them with the instructions	Greeters help	Colored instruction cards Newsprint on each table to record ideas
12:30	Continuing flow of the meeting Greeting of board members A short inspirational poem	Chairperson Ms. K.	Grooks No. 5 Piet Hein (see Bibliography)
12:35	Request by chair for each table to report 2 important suggestions for bd. meeting improvement	Chair	Collection of 5 newsprint records of suggestions
12:45	Discussion of the reports & agreement that a temp. subcommittee of 3 read the other items & come up with suggestions for improvement for the next bd. meetings	Chair	Collection of 5 newsprint records of suggestions
1:00	Present the minutes and discuss	Chair & Sec.	Extra copies of minutes
1:10	Nominations Comm. reports on its idea for broadening bd. membership. Gen. discussion of added suggestions.	Nom. Chairperson	Copies of suggestions available

Time	Activity and Methods	Who resp. for what	Arrangements & Resources room, mat., equipment
1:15	Budget discussion illustrated with pictures of present & situation—and future needs (on overhead transparencies) Table groups discuss & list questions—they star their key questions & ask them—get answers from finance comm.	Finance Chairperson & 1 finance committee member 4 finance comm. members	Overhead projector with transparency Newsprint
1:30	Vote on size of budget request	Finance chairperson	
1:35	Each table group is asked to skim again over the already mailed-out-to-them affirmative action proposal—then discuss—and are requested to formulate their table recommendations	Chairperson of task force	Pads of paper, pens
1:50	Report progress & ask questions by table groups	Same as above	
2:45	Ending of Meeting Agree to continue to discuss affirmative action recommendations next bd. meeting and the comm. will summarize the recommendations so far. Volunteers are requested for Future Planning Committee. Agreement on next meeting time and place. Thank you to group and to agenda participants.	Chairperson future planning	Collect all recorded mat. for full record of the meeting

Follow-up Actions:
- Reminder to temporary subcommittee on summary of bd. improvement suggestions memo sent to them by chair.
- Affirmation chairperson sets date with task force to read, analyze the rec., & plan strategy for next bd. meeting—maybe even a summary mailing just before the next meeting.
- Secretary gathers recorded material to include in the expanded minutes.
- Budget committee chairperson sets a meeting to discuss and implement board actions.
- The bd. chairperson asks several bd. members to meet and look at bd. improvement suggestions after they are summarized to decide which of these could be implemented at the next bd. meeting.

Preplanning Sheet		
Participants/members, their char. & needs	**Desirable Outcomes of this meeting**	**Ideas for activities, exper., resources, facilities**
• 3 students from marketing class at the university • Pat—new member—attending first meeting • Stan—experienced, critical member • Phil—50ish • Betty—65 yrs. old, enthusiastic—new • Alan—experienced, helpful, good actor • Bob—young dancer and director • Edna—new—never attended before	1. To hear report of marketing survey* 2. Decision on promotion flyer** 3. Fund-raising ideas identified 4. Decide on ways for board to select 6 plays for next season 5. Contacts identified to recruit behind-the-scene persons	Seated at round table; check for another room or space for small-group work Visual way to present marketing report Brainstorm Small group to work on how board can decide*** Have data on past plays—by cost/number in cast/type
Summary of Desired Outcomes: To hear report from marketing survey;* have promotion flyer format approved;** get a lot of ideas for board talk of deciding on 6 plays.*** To have Pat and Edna feel good about involvement.		

Planning Sheet			
Time	Activity and Methods	Who resp. for what	Arrangements & resources, room mat., equipment
7:00	The Beginning Check arrangements, directional signs to meeting, place name tags or tents ready to use	Betty	1 table which can seat 10 persons
7:15	Meet with Pat to bring him up to date on committee plans	Bob	
7:45	Marketing students & professor arrive & receive welcome and name tags (tents)	Betty	Tape or thumbtacks to put up marketing sheets
Flow of the meeting after start-up			
8:00	Review agenda and recording actions taken	Edna	Agenda on newsprint
8:03	Marketing survey report and recommendations. Questions and answers. Make plans to share report with board.	Students & staff person from univ.	Thank them for coming and invite them to report at next board meeting. Invite them to stay for rest of meeting.
8:40	Promotion folder. Presentation of sample layouts with casts. Decision on best layout.	Bob & Pat	
8:55	Decide on ways for board to determine the plays we will do next year. Review way done this past year.	Alan	(15 minutes) Groups of three to work on improving selection method
9:10	Small groups report back and select best	Phil & Edna	Newsprint for brainstorming
9:20	Fund-raising ideas. All brainstorm selection of 5 best. Share with funding committee.		Newsprint, pens
9:35	Review decisions made. Set date, time, and place of next meeting. Adjourn.	Edna	

Follow-up Actions:

Action Steps, Decisions	Who	When
Thank-you notes to marketing students	Betty	
Have promotion folder printed	Bob & Pat	Not later than 6 weeks from today
Prepare play information for board meeting selection	Alan	By board meeting
Share funding ideas with Funding Committee	Phil & Edna	Before their next meeting

Music-Center Volunteer Meeting, 9:15 a.m.—1 p.m.

Planning Sheet				
Time	Activity	Method	Who Respons.	Arrangements, Resources, Materials, Equipment, etc.
9:15	The Beginning Why am I a music-center volunteer?	Table talk and writing	Consultant	Table tents, numbers on tables, red & black pens, newsprint
9:45	Informal reporting	Participating dialogue	Consultant	
10:00	Introduction(s): Instructor, others		Chair	
10:15	4-5 "Excitements in the Volunteer World"	Lecturette in several parts	Consultant	Tape recorder
10:45	Ideating: • Recruiting • Motivating • Maintenance	Brainstorming: instruction, brain-storming, wander & vote	Consultant	Newsprint, masking tape
11:30	Lunch	Table talk: characteristics of productive boards		
12:00 noon	Board's evaluation Closing		Consultant Chair	Give back idea sheets
1:00	Linger longer			

				Arrangements, Resources, Materials,
Time	Activity	Method	Who Respons.	Equipment, etc.
Planning Sheet, Day I				
8:30	The Beginning Greet/meet/seat, discuss report	Small-group discussion: Volunteer excitements we know of in our city		Tables—mixed seating, newsprint, large felt-tip pens, tape, name tags
9:15	Introductions		Chair	
9:30	Volunteer world updated	Input with group participation	Consultant	
10:15	Skills needed to participate in not-for-profit agencies	Table work, list, discuss	Consultant	Paper, pens
10:40	Skills each person brings	Table work: Inventory by name	Consultant	5 x 7 cards
11:00	Prioritizing of skills	Vote and wander		Newsprint, large pens, tape
11:30	Pulling together needed skills with extant skills	Summary remarks	Consultant	
12:15	Lunch	New seating; meet new persons		
1:45	Meeting and presentation skills needed by leaders in volunteer agencies	Lecturette with discussion Brainstorm on all the characteristics of productive meetings	Consultant	*Doldrums* book
3:30	Break			
3:45 to 4:30	The not-for-profit board now and onward	Exchange of experiences: • Chair • Group • Comments by instructor		

Planning Sheet, Day II				
Time	Activity	Method	Who Respons.	Arrangements, Resources, Materials, Equipment, etc.
8:30	Leadership skills needed by board members in the not-for-profit agency	Table discussion	Instructor Others	
9:30	Realistic future planning	Explain simplified process; *total* group work on a specific goal selected by group (table Force Fields)	Instructor	From Goals to Action
10:30	Ways to help agencies grow and change	Decreasing resistance to: 1. new people 2. new ideas Brainstorm		
11:10 to 11:30	Tie up and evaluation			Give back idea sheets: 1. Things/ideas you found helpful in this seminar 2. Suggestions for improvements 3. Specific skills you would like to improve

How to Teach: Facilitating Learning, 2 Days

Planning Sheet, Day I			
Time	**Activity and Methods**	**Who Respons.**	**Arrangements, Resources, Equipment, Materials, etc.**
7:30	Breakfast		
8:00	Introductions and announcements		
8:15	Opening remarks	Instructor	
8:30 8:45	Table discussions: Recall, reflect, share some meaningful, important learning experiences that have stayed with you. Why? Some report out	Instructor	
9:00	Input: Overview of the two days	Instructor	
9:15	What are some of the problems and concerns in regard to the teaching-learning process that you hope we will deal with? Discuss and list on newsprint, hang up, comment.	Instructor	Newsprint, felt-tipped pens, tape
10:15	Break		
10:30	Problem-solving groups Making change happen in your settings: • How does it occur now? Additional ideas • Starts in other parts of hierarchy • In your arena: You make changes that work and word gets around, sharing successes, encouraging students to share and make suggestions. • Student-faculty retreats, meetings • Curriculum committees on which you serve or volunteer to serve • Be clear about the reason(s) for change.	Instructor	
11:30	Lunch		
12:45	Force Field Analysis as a tool for making change; input by instructor; do it	Instructor	From Goals to Action

Planning Sheet, Day I, continued			
Time	Activity and Methods	Who Respons.	Arrangements, Resources, Equipment, Materials, etc.
1:15	Input by instructor: How to teach, my beliefs and assumptions Total group: Brainstorm "all the ways to facilitate learning"	Instructor	Pens, paper, newsprint
2:00	Report out; discuss	Instructor	Pens, paper, newsprint
2:30	Divide total group into table groups; each group will select and deal with one of the following subjects: • Making uninteresting subject matters interesting • Communicating sense of pride, ethics, responsibility • Motivating students to become more independent and responsible, self-confident • All the ways to deal with students who don't measure up • How to deal with problem students	Instructor	Pens, paper, newsprint
3:15	Report out; discuss	Instructor	Pens, paper, newsprint
3:45 to 4:00	All the methods we have used today so far: a brief summary	Instructor	

Planning Sheet, Day II			
Time	Activity and Methods	Who Respons.	Arrangements, Resources, Equipment, Materials, etc.
7:15	Total group divided into ten con-sultation/design groups Some transition comments, and purpose and overview of day: (a) to practice hands-on planning and designing a learning event with some new and different elements included; (b) to do one to be used "back home"	Instructor	*Doldrums:* Planning Sheet No. 1 (Diagnostic Planning), and *Doldrums:* Planning Sheet No. 2 (The Meeting Design)
7:30	Explain Planning Sheet No. 1 Do Planning Sheet No. 1	Instructor	Planning Sheet No. 1
8:30	Report out; discuss problems/alter-natives/who else *might* be involved in planning	Instructor	Planning Sheet No. 1
8:45	Explain Planning Sheet No. 2 Do Planning Sheet No. 2	Instructor	Planning Sheet No. 2
9:45	Report out; discuss; critique	Instructor	Planning Sheet No. 2
10:00	Design an actual learning event for "back-home" use in two phases: 1. Diagnostic planning 2. The actual meeting design		
11:30	Report out; discuss; critique	Instructor	Planning Sheets No. 1 and No. 2
11:45	Make changes in planning/design of event	Instructor	Planning Sheets No. 1 and No. 2
12:00	Lunch		

Planning Sheet, Day II (continued)			
Time	Activity and Methods	Who Respons.	Arrangements, Resources, Equipment, Materials, etc.
1:00	New groups: Learning contracts • elements • who is doing it now Individually: jot down a learning contract	Instructor	Newsprint, felt-tipped pens, paper, pens
1:30	All the ways to be a facilitator All the ways to be a resource All the ways to be a connector Brainstorm three roles; identify value	Instructor	Newsprint, felt-tipped pens, paper, pens
2:00	Report out and general discussion	Instructor	
2:15	Break		
2:45	Individual: Brainstorm all your plus-and-minus feelings re teaching	Instructor	Newsprint, felt-tipped pens, paper, pens
3:00	Select the key positives and key negatives of your feelings re teaching role	Instructor	
3:10	Whole-group vote on key plus and minus	Instructor	
3:20	Divide into new table groups and each group select one key minus and work on how to overcome or reduce that point Explain: Force Field	Instructor	From Goals to Action
3:45	Report out; discuss	Instructor	
4:00 to 4:30	Review and summary of all methods used in both days Ideas out		

Planning/Design Sheet	
Time	**Activity**
8:30	Discuss the best, most wonderful meetings you have been in. What made them good? Discuss the most awful meetings. What made them bad? List on newsprint
8:45	Report out or look at them together. List key questions/items you would like to have included today.
9:00	Introduction of consultant Consultant: Objectives of the day
9:15	Why all this current interest in effective, productive meetings? Group and consultant Some beliefs about meetings. Consultant
9:30	Brainstorm (give rules) 1. All the characteristics of a productive meeting 2. All the reasons to have a meeting 3. All the characteristics of an unproductive meeting
10:00	Hang up newsprint sheets; vote on most important ingredients; discuss.
10:15	Leadership: Think of a leader you admire. Think of three reasons why. Discuss and list the qualities. Report out.
11:00	Situations we find hard to handle: List specific problems. Practice and use: Behavioral skills practice steps
12:00	Lunch
1:15	Designing and planning your meetings (Use tools and planning charts in this book.) Choose one to plan. Regroup. Critique and revise plan.
3:00 to 3:30	Discuss: Odd items from expectation list. Methods we have used. Comments/debrief.

A Sample Physical Arrangements Briefing Sheet

You may need a copy of this for the custodian, or the hotel or motel liaison, and/or for your Subcommittee on Arrangements (as well as for yourself). Be sure to keep a copy of whatever you send or give out.

Time of meeting

      Beginning:

      Ending:

Date:

Place or Space:

Number of People:

Equipment: mike(s), easels, projectors, screens, video, VCR, etc.:

Kinds and number of tables:

Chair/pillow arrangements:

Directional signs; bulletin board listings; directions to meeting:

Arrangement: (please draw)

It would be helpful to draw a diagram of the physical setup you desire for your meeting. Figures 1 and 2 give two examples:

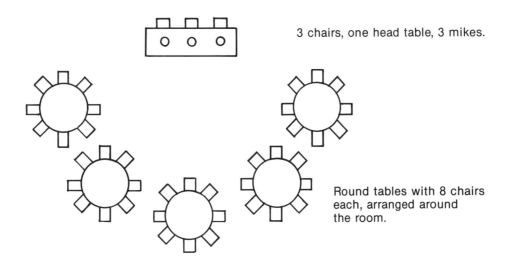

3 chairs, one head table, 3 mikes.

Round tables with 8 chairs each, arranged around the room.

Figure 1. Setup for Forty People

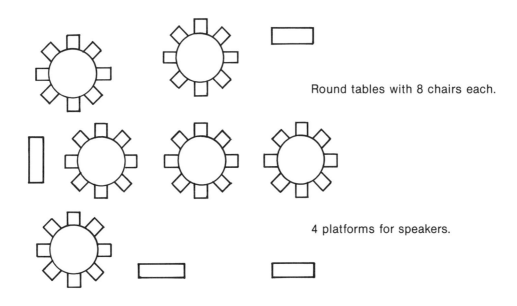

Round tables with 8 chairs each.

4 platforms for speakers.

Figure 2. Setup with Speakers' Platforms and No Head Table

An Illustrative Agenda Sheet

Most groups use an "old business—new business" type of agenda. We would like to suggest another format which is one that involves participants in a different way and makes the agenda into a work sheet. The following columns can be used, and a form is provided for the agenda work sheet.

1. Timing. Indicate the amount of time a given item will take (e.g., 15, treasurer's report and discussion) so you can see whether or not the number of items can be handled in the time you have available. Or, you need to cut something out or lengthen the meeting.

2. Agenda Item. This refers to the place or order of the particular item to be dealt with (e.g., minutes, nominating committee report, by-laws discussion, etc.).

3. Method. This refers to how each item will be handled (e.g., report, total-group discussion, small-group discussion, film, brainstorming, etc.)

4. Who responsible. This refers to the name or initials of the person responsible for that item (e.g., Henry for greetings and prayer, Judy for opening remarks and call to order, etc.).

5. Resources, Materials. Here for each agenda item you list the necessary resources and materials (e.g., coffee, tea, newsprint, scratch paper, pens, name tags, pins, minutes from last meeting, etc.).

6. Disposition. Each item has a specific disposition. These include: information, inspiration, reporting, policy making, decision making, discussion, recommending. Indicate for each item what its disposition is and this will help indicate the time needed on the agenda.

7. Follow-up Actions. The column should indicate for each item what, if any, follow-up action is indicated. If there is none, it helps to write in the word "none."

8. Who. The people who will do follow-up actions should be listed with by-when dates.

Agenda Work Sheet

Meeting:

Date:

Time:

Place:

Purpose(s) or desired outcome(s) of this meeting:

Timing (1)	Agenda Item (2)	Method for presenta- tions, etc. (3)	Who responsible (4)	Resources, Materials (5)	Disposition (6)	Follow-up Actions (7)	Who (8)

TOOL KIT B: BEGINNINGS OF MEETINGS

Beginnings of meetings are important because they set a climate for and give a feeling about the meeting to the participants. They can help make people feel glad they came because the setting is organized, warm, and ready. Also, it helps to have beginnings that can start when people get there, rather than some people having to wait for others. There are many ways to begin; we give a few sample ideas here.

1. Greeting Sheet. This is a large piece of paper or cardboard that has greetings and beginning instructions on it (e.g., "Hello—Good morning! Please help yourself to tea or coffee and sit with 2 or 3 people you don't know to get acquainted. Please talk about what you hope this meeting will accomplish.").

2. Paired Interview. As soon as two people have arrived, they are asked via a greeting sheet, or verbally, or with instruction sheets, to interview each other. Each pair is provided with two file folders, and they record each other's information on the folders. The questions might be: name; kind of job you do; things that turn you on in life; that turn you off in life; hopes from this experience.

When both folders are finished, both people wear their own around their necks and walk around to meet, greet, and interact with the other participants.

You can adapt for later resource utilization whatever information you might like (e.g., special skills people have and/or special needs, etc.). These folders can then be posted alphabetically on the wall and become a resource inventory for the group. If the group is large it helps to take Polaroid pictures of all participants and paste each person's picture on the file folder—great for identification purposes. Also post them alphabetically.

3. Name Tags. Name tags can be varied in size, shape, color, simplicity and/or complexity—here are a few ideas:

- Use 3 x 5 cards with pins and have people write their name and favorite hobby.
- Use colored paper and let people cut out and fill out their own.
- Put out a variety of paper, pictures, scissors, pens, glue, etc., and encourage people to make a collage of their name.
- Be sure name tags are large and legible.

4. Sign-In Sheet. Make a large wheel listing all the functional parts of a typical community and have people sign their names in each part of the wheel to see what parts of your community are represented. (See Figure 3.) An organizational sign-in sheet could have names of departments or functions printed between the spokes of the wheel.

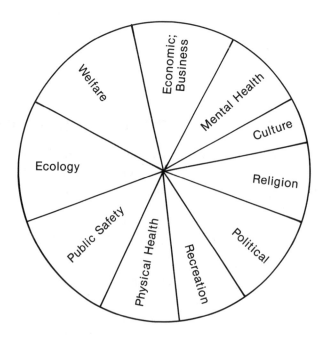

Labels on the wheel (clockwise from top): Economic; Business, Mental Health, Culture, Religion, Political, Recreation, Physical Health, Public Safety, Ecology, Welfare

Figure 3. Sign-In Sheet

---

5. Individual Identification Sheets. Post one large sheet of paper on the wall for each participant:

- If possible, put each one's name on the sheets.
- As they come in, give them each a felt pen and ask them to fill out their own sheet according to the instructions.
- Have a large instruction sheet, or run off individual sheets with instructions, so people can begin as they arrive.
- The kinds of things they might answer are:
  - name
  - favorite activities
  - things they could help others with
  - things they need help with

Now perhaps these ideas will trigger others in you. Just take time to plan your beginnings. This effort will be translated into a better and more productive meeting.

TOOL KIT C: LOOKING AT PROCESS AND PARTICIPATION

One of the most effective procedures for improving the productivity and satisfaction of any meeting is to use one or more of the available procedures for helping the group review their own working process and make decisions about ways they would like to make their work more satisfying and productive.

Such "process checks" may take no more than 10 minutes, and the saving is many times this. Here are four ways used most frequently to review the work process.

1. A "stop session" tool is used to help a group quickly collect data on "how they are doing" and to make decisions about what improvements they would like to make. See some samples of such tools in this tool kit.

2. When the agenda is developed, an item about midpoint in the agenda is entitled "taking a look at how we're doing." The leader asks the group to share diagnoses and help with ideas for improvement.

3. An outside consultant, or a member of the group, is asked to serve as a process observer and to make observations when he or she sees an opportunity to make comments that will help the group become aware of blocks in communication or possible alternative procedures that might be helpful.

4. A fourth procedure is an end-of-meeting feedback instrument that permits participants to give reactions to the meeting as a basis for improving the process of the next session. A sample of such an end-of-meeting sheet is provided in this tool kit.

Brief Stop-Action Check

To help improve our productivity, respond to the following questions.

1. How do you feel about how you are being listened to?

```
|_____|_____|_____| (please check)
very            fairly          just            somewhat
satisfied       satisfied       so-so           dissatisfied
```

Please comment on why you checked where you did:

2. How fully do you think you have been listening to and using the ideas of the others?

very	pretty	not too	quite
fully	well	well	poorly

(please check)

Please comment on why you checked where you did:

3. Please share your data with each other and agree on an idea or two on how you might improve the group's work as you continue.

Communication and Group Productivity: A Quick Check

1. What barriers to communication, if any, seem to be operating in this meeting? (Please name one or more.)

2. What can be done to improve group productivity now? (List one or more ideas.)

3. Please share your thoughts on the two questions and decide what the group might do to improve the way you work and think together.

End-of-Meeting Feedback Thoughts

1. How do you feel about what we accomplished in this meeting?

```
|_____|_____|_____| (please check)
very                fairly                  somewhat              quite
satisfied           satisfied               dissatisfied          dissatisfied
```

Please comment on reasons for checking where you did:

2. How do you feel about the way we worked on our tasks?

|_____|_____|_____| (please check)
very   fairly   somewhat   quite
satisfied   satisfied   dissatisfied   dissatisfied

Please comment on reasons for checking where you did:

3. What are suggestions for our next meeting? Procedures? Agenda? Physical arrangements?
   Leadership? or anything else.

Evaluation Sheet No. 1

1. What things were most helpful to you during this workshop? Please list.

2. Why were these things helpful to you?

3. What was least helpful?

4. Why was this so?

5. Would you like a follow-up to this workshop planned? If yes, what do you want to have included?

6. Other comments:

And what did you learn about yourself as a leader at the conference?

Well, I learned:

And what have you learned about yourself in relation to your group?

I learned:

What is something you think you will do differently now?

Next week I think I'll try:

Evaluation Sheet No. 3

1. How relevant was this session to my here-and-now needs?

|_____|_____|_____| (please check)
highly   fairly   slightly   not very
relevant   relevant   relevant   relevant

Why did you rate this as you did?

2. How probable do you think it is that you will put into action any ideas from the session?

|_____|_____|_____| (Please check)
highly   quite   slightly   not very
probable   probable   probable   probable

Why did you rate this as you did?

3. What do you think might be an outcome in your back-home situation (if any)?

4. Please give any feedback comments to the leader(s) of this meeting (e.g., about leadership style, design of the meeting, content of session, your feelings, etc.).

TOOL KIT D: GETTING IDEAS OUT AND SHARED

There are many ways to help group participants "uncork" and share their ideas. Here are some that we have found particularly useful in a wide variety of situations. Included are: brainstorming, small-group techniques, self-inquiry method, and exchange of successful practices.

1. Brainstorming!

The purpose of this method is to get out as many ideas, on a given question or problem, as possible, utilizing all the resources of the group without stopping to discuss or judge the worth of any of the ideas during the actual brainstorming session.

The time required varies from 10 to 20 minutes depending on the size of the group and the complexity of the question.

The size of the group we find best is between three and 15 persons. One person can brainstorm alone and sometimes two people can do well if this seems necessary or desirable.

Recording the ideas is very important. One person can do this or the responsibility can be shared. It helps to have large sheets of flip-chart paper and a broad-tip felt pen, so that the ideas can be seen going on the sheet and can be easily read afterward.

The question to be brainstormed about must be one to which all the participants can speak, e.g.,

- all the ways to recruit volunteers
- all the ways to improve our meetings
- all the ways to give information other than through speakers, etc.

There are four rules that help group members to do productive brainstorming. Have these rules available to the group through a verbal listing and/or posting them in easily seeable written form:

1. List all the ideas anyone has.
2. Do not discuss.
3. Do not judge—all ideas are go!
4. Repetitions are O.K. (just put the idea down again).

A helpful hint is to say to the group that if they hit a plateau or silent periods: "Just enjoy your silences because often the best ideas come after the silence."

After the brainstorming session it is possible to do a variety of things with the product(s). For instance:

1. Encourage group members to look over their list and star the four or five priority items and report those.
2. If several groups are brainstorming the same question, put the lists on the wall with masking tape and have participants mill and read each other's and mark on each other's sheets those they find most exciting or feel are priorities.
3. Or, have them check all the items they feel they could do easily (such as ways to improve their meetings).

4. You'll find other uses.

Just be sure that there is a use made of the brainstorming product(s). Most people love to brainstorm and enjoy seeing their ideas recognized and utilized. It is one of the best ways to help nonparticipants become active.

2. Small-Group Techniques

Buzz Groups. Here two or three persons "buzz"—talk for a short period of time in response to an instruction from the leader like:

List:

- Your questions about what you've just heard
- Your ideas on how to help shy people participate
- Your ideas on how we can improve our group's productivity

Small Work Groups vary in size from three to seven or eight persons. Members are requested verbally and/or in written instructions to do a particular task or set of tasks. For example:

- Members are asked to list their goals for this meeting and then to mark priorities on their list.
- Each work group has a different question to answer or problem to solve.
  —ways to recruit employees
  —ways to train employees
  —ways to keep employees happy
- Sometimes each work group is asked to brainstorm something (e.g., all the things a good leader does to help the group; all the ways to design our annual meeting, etc.).

When a group is divided into subgroups to do work, there is usually a need to report the results of each group's work and ideas. There is a variety of ways to do this. Here are some:

1. Each group reports out verbally their two favorite or best ideas. When each group has had a chance to do this other ideas can be added.
2. Reports are written out on newsprint and hung on the wall for the others to read. This makes for a useful "break" time since people can pick up a cup of coffee, go to the lavatory, etc., in addition to milling and reading.
3. Verbal reporting from each group, with one person recording the ideas on a large sheet of paper or on a transparency on an overhead projector for all to see.
4. Reproduce enough copies for every participant.
5. Give the reports to a summarizing committee who will integrate and summarize all the ideas.
6. Ask each group to make a nonverbal report of their best idea.
7. Report out and share results via a picture, collage, or paper bag puppets.

3. Self-Inquiry Method

This is a way to help participants to work by themselves and to focus on some particular item of content. The purpose may be to help them think through something before discussing it in a group (see the following self-inquiry sheets as examples).

Self-Inquiry: Anticipations and Predictions

As you look around the circle of your group, which is about to begin working together, please reflect on and jot down ideas on the two questions below:

1. What are some of the factors which you feel exist in a new group like this that will block free and open communication?

2. What initiatives might a member like yourself take to help the group begin removing such blocks to communication?

Please share some of your self-inquiry reflections with fellow group members for a few minutes.

GROUP SELF-EVALUATION

Circle the number that best describes your response to each question.

YOUR PARTICIPATION

1. Compared to other members of the group, how would you describe your participation in discussions?

   Very high   10   9   8   7   6   5   4   3   2   1   Very low

2. Compared to other members of the group, how influential have you been in the decision-making process?

   Highly influential 10   9   8   7   6   5   4   3   2   1   Little influence

GROUP EFFECTIVENESS

3. How clear are the group's role and function?

   Very clear   10   9   8   7   6   5   4   3   2   1   Very fuzzy

4. How does the leadership work?

   Shared by all   10   9   8   7   6   5   4   3   2   1   Dominated by one

5. How are important issues handled?

   Efficiently   10   9   8   7   6   5   4   3   2   1   Avoided

6. How is preparation handled?

   Efficiently   10   9   8   7   6   5   4   3   2   1   Poorly

7. How is the communication of ideas?

   Open and easy   10   9   8   7   6   5   4   3   2   1   Little listening

8. How are people accepted?

   Respectfully   10   9   8   7   6   5   4   3   2   1   Lots of rejection

9. What is the group climate?

   Mutual trust   10   9   8   7   6   5   4   3   2   1   Hostility

10. What is the group's productivity?

    Very high   10   9   8   7   6   5   4   3   2   1   Very low

The purpose of the "Internal Society" sheet is to give the participant a chance to think about how she/he feels about something, to give insight.

Our "Internal Society" and Our "Invisible Committee"

Whenever we face a decision to try something new, there is an internal dialog which starts up inside us (parts of ourselves that feel and think one way and other parts of us that feel and think differently). Also, we become aware that there are other persons in our lives who are influential reactors to our ideas and actions. As you think about changes you want to make, it will be helpful to do these two internal inquiries for a few minutes:

Internal Dialog	Invisible Committee Reactions
What do the various voices inside you say about your new change ideas, pro and con?	Who are the persons and groups whom you can visualize as supporting or questioning or rejecting your new ideas? What are they saying?

These are just a few ideas. You can adapt these to your own needs and invent new ones that help translate your designs and hopes for outcomes into a fun meeting.

4. Sharing and Integrating Ideas

It is important to remember that the reporting, sharing, and integrating activities should be brief, varied, interesting, and useful.

5. Exchange of Successful Practices

The invention of useful social practices is not unusual. New ways to greet or group people, ideas for motivating the apathetic, a novel room arrangement, etc., are all social inventions that should be useful to more people than just the inventor. Yet, such practices are rarely shared in a way that the next person can really adopt or adapt them.

Nonsharing is due to many reasons, ranging from lack of knowing how to do so, to modesty about one's own ideas, to possessiveness, to fear of rejection, to high competitiveness.

We have found that people like to share new ideas when they are given some help to do a productive job of it. Here is a format to guide you; you will want to adapt it to your needs.

Usually each person in the group is given the interview form. Then the leader asks each person to share one practice that has worked for him/her on some agreed-on topic (e.g., "ways I've motivated people to participate in meetings," or "ways I've helped kids learn," etc.). Everyone who has a successful practice on this topic mentions what it is. Someone writes the topic with the contributor's name on a large sheet of paper. After everyone who wants to contribute an idea has done so, the group votes on the priority ones they want to hear about in detail. These are starred and then the first exchange-of-practice interview begins. Questions are asked in the order on the form. One person records the answers and has them duplicated as soon as each interview is finished.

It is possible to record the answers directly for reproduction with enough copies for everyone, or participants can take their own notes on the form.

Exchange of Practices Interview Form

Name of "Inventor"

Address of "Inventor"

Telephone

1. What is the practice?

2. Describe it so the listeners can see it in their mind's eye (give steps involved in doing it).

3. Where and with whom can it be used?

4. Facilities needed:

5. Costs:

6. Problems to watch for:

7. Any evaluation of it? What?

8. Adaptations? (Of the practicer or anyone else in the group.)

6. From Goals to Action: Participative Planning

A. *Assumptions Underlying This Approach*

1. Persons to be affected by plans and decisions should have a part in making these plans and decisions.
2. Such involvement leads to an investment of interest, time, and responsibility on the part of the participants.
3. This process requires the selection of realistic "do-able" goals.
4. It is a way of working toward something, rather than getting away from pain or problems.
5. The phases of brainstorming stimulate creativity because of the nonjudgmental, free atmosphere for getting ideas out.
6. There are no preconceived ways to reach the goal.
7. There is an emphasis on alternatives all the way through the process—alternative goals and alternative action patterns.
8. Since the work is done in a group there is much opportunity to build on each other's ideas.
9. There is orderly movement from image of potentiality brainstorming, to goal selection, to diagnosing of forces that will help or hinder the reaching of the goal, to alternative actions on the strongest forces, to beginning start-up action steps.

B. *Images of Potentiality*

1. In this process you take an imaginary leap five years, or one year, or six months, etc., ahead and look at what is *now* happening that makes you pleased with the progress since five years, one year, or six months ago. You brainstorm and list *all* the images you see. You do this in the present tense.
2. *Example:* "It is now _____ , and you are floating in a helicopter above your department, district office, branch, service, or office. As you look down at *your area of work* you are pleased with the improved communication you see going on. Specifically, what do you see?"
    - "Easy access by employees to the boss."
    - "Productive, fun, short staff meetings."
    - "Clear understanding and use of program goals by most employees."
    - "More involvement in decision making."
    - "Etc."
3. After the group gets out *all* the possible images, the members look back at the list and choose the one that they feel is most important to achieve, and that they would like to work on. If the group is large (over seven people), choose two images and divide the group to do the work on both simultaneously.
4. Now translate the image into a goal on which you will work (e.g., to involve more employees in decision making).

C. Force-Field Analysis[1]

1. Discuss and list *all* the things—all the forces—that you know will help you reach the goal. These are things that are now in the picture (in the field) that will be driving (+) forces toward the goal.

2. Then do the same for blocks or restraining forces (−).

3. If a force is neither clearly a help or a hindrance, make a third column marked "?" and then it can be determined later how to find out whether these "?" forces are + or − or both.

4. *Example:* (See also Force Field under C-6.)

Goal: To Involve More Employees in Decision Making.

Helps +	Blocks −	?
1. Some supervisors want help in decision making. 2. In our organization there is a trend toward participatory management. 3. It has been successfully tried in some areas. 4. Etc.	1. There is little history of participatory decision making in the department. 2. Many supervisors lack skill in involving employees. 3. Some decisions need to be made immediately. 4. It takes time. 5. Etc.	1. The attitude of top management. 2. The willingness to change on part of present supervisors. 3. Etc.

5. When all the driving (+) and restraining (−) forces have been listed, plot them on a force field. As you plot them you will need to decide on the *strength of each force.* How big or how important are the forces in relation to reaching or blocking your goal attainment? It is possible that some forces will be both plus and minus, but they are not likely to have the same strengths.

6. *Example:* (See also C-4 above.)

Goal: To Involve More Employees in Decision Making.

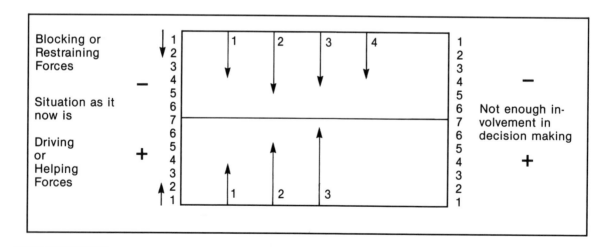

[1]Based on the concept of Kurt Lewin. See *Field Theory in Social Science* by K. Lewin, 1951. Chicago: University of Chicago Press.

7. After listing all the forces you can think of and plotting them on the force field, these are your action choices:

    a. Take the strongest negative force or forces that you can do something about, and brainstorm all the things you could do to diminish or demolish it or them.

    b. Strengthen the strongest positives (again, brainstorm all the ways to do this).

    c. Combine strong positives, if possible.

    d. Reverse a strong negative into a strong positive.

    e. Remove forces, if possible.

8. The best payoff usually is to diminish the strongest "do-able" negative force(s). So, let us start there. *Brainstorm all* the alternative actions you could take here, and *select/star* those that seem feasible as first steps.

D. Action Strategies

1. Now look back over this list, and from the preliminary selections choose those actions that you can take to start your work to decrease the selected restraining force.

2. To begin on, you may wish to select one or several.

3. On the selection of your beginning entry steps, answer very specifically these questions:

    a. Besides us, *whom else do we need* to work on this?

    b. *Where* do we begin?

    c. *How* do we begin? (Phone call, meeting, letter, etc.)

    d. *Who* will do what to get us started?

    e. *When* do we meet again? *Where? Who* will be the temporary convenor?

7. Ideas for Effective Work Teams

The following notes and the lists of do's and don'ts should be helpful in the care and feeding of work groups.

Your energy and your teamwork as work groups in planning, acting, and activating others is the heart of a cooperative staff team. The successes from our collective efforts will be many, and the most important cause of each success will be the creativity and energy of a work group. That's why the success of your work group—of each work group—is so important.

So becoming and being a productive successful work group is a great challenge—and not an easy one. Teaming up to get things done that nobody can do alone is difficult, demanding, personally rewarding, and fun. So the purpose of this brief memo to you is to identify the things each and all of us can do to create and maintain vital productive work groups.

Please use these notes as an agenda for building your group, a tool for improving your productivity, a check list of "do's" and "don'ts." The notes are based on the successful and unsuccessful experiences of many work groups.

Some Very Important "Do's"

1. Narrow your "mission" down to a very do-able first goal. Next goals will follow as a solid first goal is accomplished.

2. Be sure someone is responsible for *planning* your meeting, so your collective time together will be well used.

3. Always be thinking about what additional persons you need to add as resources for your action—and decide on who should recruit with what strategy of approach.

4. Always be thinking about division of labor in getting the work done—who can best do what?

5. Keep giving yourselves deadlines, and help each other keep them.

6. Clarify your needs for help—the kinds of support you need—and ask your leaders for the help you need. That is a sign of strength: to know what you need, when, whom to ask for it, and how.

7. Consider whether co-leadership might not make things go better and how you might rotate leadership over time.

8. *Keep good records of your meetings, your decisions, your actions, your contacts, your accomplishments.* This is very important for keeping everyone informed, for orienting new members, for clarifying and celebrating progress as a basis for asking for support.

9. Project your calendar of meetings *well ahead* instead of setting dates from meeting to meeting.

10. Pick a comfortable place to meet with good work space and facilities.

A Few Important "Don'ts"

1. The most important "don't" is: Don't start by tackling too big a goal! Define some concrete short-term goals or steps that will lead in the direction of your bigger purpose.

2. Don't try to do it with only two or three people. Put your energy and creativeness into recruiting others and get a division of labor to make things happen.

3. Don't get together for a meeting without having a plan for the meeting and what you want to come out with as results of the meeting.

4. Don't assume important people will say "no" to your requests and avoid approaching them. Just concentrate on the best strategy of getting them interested.

5. Don't assume it's better if you "do it all by yourselves." One of the greatest strengths is asking for help at the right time from the right persons. You demonstrate leadership when you ask.

Some Characteristics of a Good Meeting

1. The furniture is arranged so everyone is looking at each other.
2. There is a place to record ideas up front, preferably on a newsprint pad so it can be saved. (Chalkboards have to be erased.)
3. An agenda is presented, added to, agreed on.
4. There are time estimates of how long each agenda item should take.
5. Someone has agreed to be the recorder of the thinking and decisions of the meeting and is ready to write the notes up and get them to everyone.
6. The notes indicate who has agreed to what before the next meeting, and the names are underlined in the notes as a reminder.
7. Dates of future meetings (not just the next meeting) are set well ahead so everyone can put them on the calendar.
8. At least once or twice in every meeting someone asks, "How are we doing on our way of working today? Any ideas about how we can improve to be more productive?"
9. Usually the question will be considered, "Who else do we want to involve?"
10. Usually the last item of a good meeting is a summary of who will be doing what between then and the next meeting.

Planning the Good Meeting—and the Next One

One advantage of having a co-leader is that the two of you can do a better job than one of sitting down and planning the purpose, agenda, and flow of activity of the next meeting.

If you don't have co-leaders, then the leader should develop a practice of asking one or two members to be an informal planning team to think together ahead of time about the meeting. *A good meeting cannot just happen* without some creative-thinking time and agenda preparations.

The items to cover at this prethinking session are:

1. The best flow of the agenda.
2. What people can get started on when they walk in the door (before everyone is there). There are often things to read, some starting thinking to do, etc.
3. How to get the reports of what has happened since the last meeting.
4. How to start the discussion on each item.
5. Which items call for decisions, which ones are just information, which ones are for brainstorming but not decisions, etc.
6. Guesses as to how long each item might take, as a working plan to present to the group.
7. Who will be asked to lead off on each item.
8. Who will bring the needed supplies, take care of the coffee, etc.

And After the Meeting

While things are still fresh—that night or the next day—is the time for the very crucial "debriefing review" with your co-leader or informal planning team—over coffee or even over the phone if it is not easy to get together. You will have a better chance of improving each meeting and keeping things going strong if you have this brief post-mortem session. The agenda should be as follows:

1. How did the meeting go? How could we have improved it? What shall we try the next time to make it better?
2. What kind of follow-up on commitments do we need to plan on?

That's enough for the agenda of a post-mortem. But it's *very important!*

Using These Ideas

You will have a better chance of obtaining these ideas and making your work group stronger if the members know that each of them will receive a memo containing the ideas that were presented and that a discussion of the ideas will be on the agenda of the next meeting. If the group agrees with the ideas or adds to them, you will be building mutual expectations and support to make these expectations happen—and that's what counts.

8. Parliamentary Know-How

The following motions are grouped according to the purpose to be accomplished:[2]

- To introduce business ....move to main motion.
- To approve action.....................move to accept, adopt, or ratify.
- To modify or change ....move to amend or refer to a committee.
- To defer action.........................move to postpone to a definite time, refer to a committee, or lay on table.
- To limit discussion....................move to time debate.
- To stop discussion ....move the previous question.
- To determine correctness of an announced voice vote ....move for division of the assembly.
- To suppress a question...............object to consideration, move to postpone indefinitely, or lay on table.
- To object to decision of the chair ....move an appeal from the decision.
- To make a request ....call for point of information, rise to parliamentary inquiry, or raise question of privileges.
- To consider a second time ....move to take from the table, reconsider, or rescind.
- To repeal action........................move to rescind.

---

[2]Based on *Robert's Rules of Order, Newly Revised.* (1981). Reston, VA: National Association of Secondary School Principals.

Most-Used Motions:

Below is a list of the most-used motions.[3]

1. Main Motion: Proposal for action or for expression of certain views. Only *one* main motion may be on the floor at a time.

2. Subsidiary Motions: Motions to modify or delay action on the main motion. This is *in order* when the main motion is being discussed:

   • To Amend or modify—Five methods to amend: (1) to strike; (2) to insert; (3) to strike and insert; (4) to add at end of sentence; (5) to substitute. Substitution generally is used only for an entire paragraph or section; strike and insert is quicker and easier and accomplishes the same purpose.

   • Refer to Committee—For information, for appropriate recommendations and/or to carry out recommendations.

   • Postpone to a Certain Time—Defer further consideration of the main question until a definitely stated time.

   • Previous Question—To close debate on current question. Affirmative vote (two-thirds without discussion) closes debate and orders immediate vote on pending question. The call "Question" may be ignored by the Chair.

3. Lay on Table: Set aside temporarily. Majority vote and no discussion. Motion may not be modified. If definite time is desired, *postpone* should be employed.

4. Incidental Motions: These arise from pending question and must be decided before the question.

   • Request for Information
   • Point of Order
   • Appeal
   • Division of Assembly

   No recognition is required. Division is used by the Chair or the Assembly when the outcome of a vote is uncertain. A standing vote need *not* be counted unless the outcome is still uncertain or a record of the vote is required.

5. Reconsider: Must be made by one who voted on the prevailing side; in order *only* on the same day or the succeeding legislative day only after the vote to which it applies was taken. If reconsideration carries, the motion to which it applies is again before the Assembly.

6. Rescind or cancel: May be called for by anyone when it is too late for reconsideration if action is not under way. Two-thirds vote without notice is required; majority, if notice to rescind has been given.

7. Adjourn: May be accomplished by general consent or by motion.

---

[3]Based on *Robert's Rules of Order, Newly Revised.* (1981). Reston, VA: National Association of Secondary School Principals.

TOOL KIT E: GOAL SETTING AND ACTION PLANNING

Setting long-range and short-range goals is one of the important agenda items in many groups and their meetings. And just as important as a good process of choosing goals is the planning to take the best actions to implement these goals. From where do we get our goals? Here are eight sources of ideas for goals that we have identified:

1. Eight Sources of Goals

Goal Source 1: From Those Being Served

The needs, expectations, confrontations of those we are trying to serve through our educational efforts, i.e., the students, are a very important source of good ideas. What are signs of discontent and boredom? How are they feeling about learning? What growth are they showing or not showing?

Goal Source 2: From Significant Others

The organization is surrounded by other systems and persons who make up its environment, e.g., the economic system of business and taxpayers; the political system of voters; liberals and conservatives; youth with their ideas; the parents with their expectations, hopes, concerns; people serving agencies that can offer or withhold collaboration. They have important ideas to be considered.

Goal Source 3: From the Successful Goals of Others

Systems and groups of all kinds are also continuously projecting goals and trying to achieve them. Some have had very exciting success experiences that have relevance for us. What are they?

Goal Source 4: From Policy-Practice Discrepancies

We have previously set goals and policies. What are the discrepancies between these intentions and what we are actually doing? Closing some of these gaps could be important goals.

Goal Source 5: From Listing Our Current Problems

From such a list we select the priorities on which to work.

Goal Source 6: From Predictions About the Future

Many predictions and projections of the future are being made by futurists and long-range planners. What implications do these predictions have for our goal setting?

Goal Source 7: From Our Images of Potential

What would the best programs we can imagine look like in action? Do we agree on these?

Goal Source 8: From Our Own National Leadership

What ideas for goals and plans are in the minds of the leadership of our systems? Have they been set down in writing? How much commitment is there?

2. Discovering and Choosing Goals by Images of Potentiality[4]

A typical way that most groups set goals is to list the problems they want to do something about and to decide what the "problems" are. An analysis of this approach has uncovered several interesting facts that led us to develop another approach:

1. We discovered that when a group is listing its problems, the voices become more and more depressed.

2. More and more comments indicate a sense of impotence or futility about action taking and problem solving.

3. There are more and more comments that attribute the causes of problems to "outside forces we can't do anything about."

4. As we listened to a wide variety of groups setting goals and priorities after such a "problem census" we noted that their goal selections were oriented toward "getting away from pain (problems)" rather than "going toward some positive image of desired achievement."

As a result of this analysis we have developed a future-oriented approach to selecting action goals.

Taking a Goal-Setting Image Trip into the Future

Your work group (or committee) will be making this trip together. You need a large sheet of newsprint and a person to act as recorder who will jot down your images as you report them.

You are projecting yourselves ahead in time—a year—and making observations of what you see going on in your setting, speaking in the present tense—you are there! Be concrete in reporting what you are seeing that pleases you with what is going on.

You are not predicting what you think will or will not happen. And you are not expressing unreal fantasies. You are observing desired developments which have a sense of reality-feasibility of a highly desirable future. Be creative. Use imagination. But be realistic. O.K., here are some instructions for the trip—the focus for your observations.

Suggestions for Your Observations. It is one year hence and you are looking down from your helicopter. You are pleased with what you see. You are seeing your group working together, and the various things you have caused to happen. Describe in the present tense how your group is functioning and what is happening, because of your efforts, that pleases you. Write down all the things that you are pleased about and you can see happening. Be as concrete as possible.

Selecting a Priority Image. After your group has listed all the images of potentiality they can project, you are ready to return to the present, and in the present, review the list of potential images. The job now is to select a priority image (or possibly two) which the group agrees is the most important to achieve and which they want to plan to start work toward. If the group is as large as, e.g., fifteen to twenty-five, you will have the resources to select two priorities and divide into two subgroups for planning. You will probably use a number of criteria for choosing your priority image(s), e.g., program importance, feasibility, sense of commitment by the members of your groups, etc.

---

[4]From Fox, Lippitt, & Schindler-Rainman (1976). See Bibliography.

Translating Your Priority Image into a Goal Statement. Your desired image of the future now needs to be formulated as a goal. It is important to make your goal as clear, concise, and specific as possible. To do this, try to state it in such a way that you can know when it has been achieved; that is, the goal must be measureable and do-able. Also, it is important to set a beginning and ending time for accomplishing this goal. Most of all, the goal should be realistic. It should be something which you feel you stand a good chance of achieving. If it would be pushing your luck, or would be something very difficult to achieve in the time allotted for it, perhaps you should amend it, trim it down, clarify it further, or choose a different goal.

Two examples of a goal statement which meet these qualifications might be: (1) to start a program to train managers to work with a diverse work force, and (2) to have in place a strategic planning group with the system.

3. A Sequence of Action Planning

Diagnosis of Helps and Hindrances
(an adaptation from Kurt Lewin's Force-Field Analysis)
With your goal statement at the top of a large sheet, make a chart as illustrated below, to list all the factors (forces) you can think of that will help, support, push toward the goal (left-hand list) and all the factors (forces) that might block or hinder movement toward the goal.

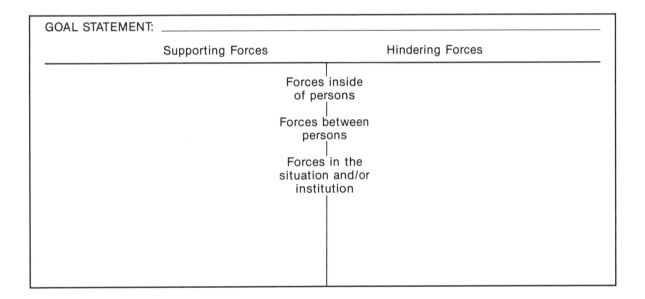

Please note we have suggested a way to clarify your forces as you list them on the chart:

1. Some forces will be factors inside yourselves and other persons (e.g., lack of skill, ambivalence, enthusiasm, or bias about importance of goal).
2. Other forces will be generated by the relations between people or the style of the group (e.g., norms against trying anything new, consensus about importance, etc.).
3. Other forces will come from the characteristics of the larger environment and institutions, such as lack of resources, budget, supportive policy.

Make as complete a list of factors as you can, realizing you may not have the data to be sure how strong some of them are—but make the best guesses you can. If there are factors you cannot now log as supportive or hindering, make a separate list of "?" items to be researched.

Brainstorming Removal of Hindrances and Mobilization of Supports

Brainstorm 1. (See brainstorm rules in Tool Kit D.) Now brainstorm all the ways to remove the hindrances you have listed. You may want to select the strongest hindrance item that you think you can do something about. Brainstorm all the ideas from that list for first action steps.

Brainstorm 2. Next, brainstorm all the ways to mobilize the supports you have listed.

Selecting Feasible Action Priorities

Look at each of the two brainstorm lists you have just produced. Discuss each list and select from each the three, four, or five items you consider priorities for action. Star or circle these items so that they are easily identifiable.

Steps of Implementation

You are now ready to move to actual action step planning. It is suggested you include the following:

1. List who besides you is needed to work on the priorities you have selected.
2. How will you recruit these persons and who will do it, when?
3. How do you begin on the action steps? What do you need to do?
4. Who will do what to get started?
5. Where to start?
6. When will the group report to each other on progress?
7. Who will convene the next meeting?

Planning for Follow-Through

It is important to have follow-up meetings to support each other; to change plans or regroup; to report progress or lack of it; to make new or additional plans. This follow-through can be done through face-to-face total group meetings; through subgroup meetings; and/or through telephone conference calls.

Try it! You might enjoy this way of working on goals and seeing your own progress on reaching them.

TOOL KIT F: ROLE PLAYING AND SKILL PRACTICE

1. Skill Practice Episodes

Some especially useful triggers and ingredients are audiotaped or written episodes from which skill practice opportunities can be developed, or you can create your own tape episodes which should always be very brief and end at a critical "what would you say now" punchline.
Here are guidelines for the flow of a skill practice exercise.

Guidelines for Skill Practice

1. Select an appropriate situation to play.
2. Read it; sometimes it helps to read it twice for your group.
3. Now, using the brainstorm rules (in Tool Kit D), brainstorm all the ways the situation could be handled.
4. From this list select one, or a combination of several, that you would like to try out.
5. Select persons to play the roles in the situation, and one to direct it.
6. Decide on a time and place where it takes place.
7. Now start with the last line—or play the whole situation as you've just heard or read it.
8. Keep going and try the method for handling you have selected. Keep going a few more sentences until the director cuts it.
9. Now discuss how it went—how the participants felt—how it could be handled even better.
10. Try the same situation again with the new suggestions. Discuss.
11. Try it as many times as you like until you feel able to handle it easily.

2. Using Role-Playing Methods[5]

Role playing is probably one of the oldest, most used, and most useful means of "laboratory learning," or learning by direct experience in a simulated, risk-free setting. In meeting and helping situations, role playing is often very helpful in working on specific, real problems in a "safe" setting—where issues can be clarified by graphic, behavioral communication; where people can learn to understand better the viewpoints of others; where new behaviors or action alternatives can be tried out with no risk of failure (or, more exactly, no negative consequences of failure). In fact, there are no mistakes and there is no failure in a role-play situation, since the examination and understanding of effective and ineffective behavior can be extremely valuable to the participants.

---

[5]Adapted from paper by Marshall Sashkin and Peggy Lippitt.

How Role Playing Gets Underway

In a role-play situation the planner, leader, consultant, or facilitator provides a clear definition of the situation, in as much detail as necessary. Often, a few words of description are enough. Individuals are then selected (or volunteer) who are cast as characters to play the various roles in acting out the situations. They are individually briefed in the parts they are to take. This may be done publicly, privately, or through prepared, written role descriptions. There may or may not be an audience; that is, in a small group everyone may be involved (though it would be generally desirable to have one or more observers), or in a large group there may be "multiple" role plays, or the role play may be performed before an audience.

The acting may be ended when the problem is clearly illustrated, may merely be interrupted for discussion and continued, or may be carried through to a natural conclusion. Discussion of the situation and learnings would follow.

Aims and Uses

While we have given a general background description of the uses of role playing, this learning method is actually suited to a variety of specific learning purposes:

1. To clarify and vividly illustrate a problem situation of some specific behavior. The role-play situation provides surprisingly vivid and real information about problems and affords an opportunity for visually examining behavior which no amount of discussion could do.

2. To provide a group with a background of common experience for discussion. A clear, shared frame of reference is very helpful for effective communication around complex issues.

3. To involve more intensely a group of individuals in a discussion situation. Either before the audience or with multiple groups, the role-play method is generally interesting and involving for participants and observers.

4. To provide an additional or alternative medium of communication and expression. To say and to do can be very different; role playing can clarify and add to what can be said in a discussion and can serve to express feelings, via behavior, which are often hard to verbalize. In addition, role playing can be used as a feedback-check or understanding of directions or instructions.

5. To help people understand a situation from the viewpoints of other persons. Role playing is one of the best ways to help people develop empathic understanding—an appreciation for the thoughts and feelings of others. Furthermore, in some situations it has been shown that the technique of role-reversal—two persons who take roles or positions opposite to their "real" positions—can lead to more positive feelings toward the other person and their position. Thus, role playing can sometimes lead to sympathy as well as empathy (or understanding). Sometimes a situation is played twice to give two different participants experience in handling the situation.

6. To give insight into the behavior of one's self and others. Through role playing, participants can find out how their behavior affects others, with no fear of any real negative consequences or reprisals. They can also gain clearer insight into the behavior of others; misconceptions can be mitigated or removed.

7. To teach new behavior through modeling. When instructed to behave in certain specified ways, new, more effective behavior can be modeled for an audience by the role players. Alternatively, the instructor or leader can model such behavior as a participant in a role-play situation.

8. To provide a no-risk setting for trying out new behavior. As well as examining the effects of present behavior, participants can experiment with new, alternative behaviors and see what the results are, with no risk of negative consequences. Also, the participants can try to express their intentions in behavior and see if they can effectively do so and if the results are as was intended.

9. To practice specific behavior skills. Students or trainees can have a realistic opportunity to practice specific behavioral skills that will improve their abilities, for example, to chair a meeting, to speak in front of a group, etc. Participants thus develop proficiency in these skills, can clearly see their progress, and can examine the results.

10. To evaluate alternative behaviors or actions. A variety of action-solutions for a problem situation can be tried out and the best behavior-actions can be clearly determined.

While all of the above uses are valuable, the most important aims or reasons for using role-play methods are generally the development of empathic understanding; understanding the effects of one's own and others' behavior; discovering new, more effective behaviors; and training and practice in specific behavior skills.

Types of Role-Play Situations

Basically there are two general methods for preparing a role play: extemporaneous, verbal definition of the situation and roles; or prepared, written briefings as to the situation and the roles.

When the role play is extemporaneous, the situation must be described very briefly and clearly, and the roles cannot be overly complex. The role players can, however, be briefed privately, if this is seen as desirable. In some ways, written roles give as much flexibility as extemporaneous preparation. More adequate role descriptions, with more complex situations, are generally possible. In general, extemporaneous role playing is most useful when the issue centers around a real or anticipated problem, while written role briefings are best for training in specific behavioral skills, which the role play can be designed to emphasize.

For either type, there are two general categories of use: on-stage role playing and multiple-group role playing. In on-stage role plays, two or more persons are involved in the role play while others present are either observers or are asked to identify with one of the actors. One advantage of this procedure is that everyone experiences the same situation, but in later discussion a variety of different interpretations are usually given, thus making for lively and potentially insightful discussion. However, if the role play takes much time, observers tend to become bored and lose interest. Thus, this method requires considerable skill on the part of the leader, in deciding when to interrupt or end the role play, or whether to "prod" the role players to "move along."

The multiple role play in small subgroups was developed by Maier and Zerfoss (1952) for use with large groups, up to forty or fifty persons. They may work either on the same or on different situations. While a high degree of involvement is generated, since everyone is a direct participant, there are some problems. For example, it often happens that groups will reach points of completion at different times. Thus, some participants may engage in private conversations, lose interest, exchange role information which it may be desirable to withhold until the discussion period, or become disruptive for those still involved in the role play. With groups of fifty or more it can be difficult to hold a good post-role-play discussion unless the group is divided into smaller discussion groups. The variety of experiences of persons in the same role situation provides rich comparative data for discussion.

Procedures

Following is the normal sequence of steps in actually using the role-play method. These steps are generally applicable to any type of role-play situation. Any printed role materials needed should, of course, be prepared well in advance.

1. The situation should be described briefly, clearly, and succinctly. This should be done even if a written description is given to the role players and/or observers, although in that case the description may be even briefer. Although we cannot go into great detail here on the design of role-play situations, the user should, in developing a role-play situation, always keep in mind the primary purpose or aim he or she has in using this method. The role play should be tailored to this purpose, with the principle of parsimony in mind; that is, use the minimum number of characters, and make any description as brief as is needed by covering only essential facts.

2. Choose the participants. Sometimes calling for volunteers is useful, but sometimes this is not desirable, since a poor performance could result in the individual's "losing face" before his or her peers. Also, it is generally important not to place a person with a specific real problem in a similar role. In many circumstances it is desirable to pre-set group composition, such as to avoid groups in which a superior-subordinate pair (in real life) have these roles reversed. While there may be times when such a reversal might be desired for a specific purpose and intent, this should not be allowed by chance.

3. Brief the actors. When written roles are used, allow adequate time for all participants to finish reading. It is not generally desirable to provide written roles that are so long and complex that the role players need to be given them to read over and study beforehand. Allow time for any questions. When the briefing is verbal be sure to check whether the participants clearly understand their roles. It is generally helpful to tell participants to simply make up any information they need which was not covered in the briefing, but to avoid making up facts just for the sake of doing so. If necessary, the participants can be given a few suggestions as to how to behave.

4. Assign tasks to the audience or observers. When there is an audience, or when individuals are assigned to observe in a role-play group (for multiple role playing), it is generally helpful to assign specific tasks. Sometimes part of the audience or certain observers can be asked to identify with one or another of the role players, acting as alter-egos or advisors. Or, printed observers' sheets can be used with brief instructions on what to watch for and keep track of (e.g., "note how many times each person speaks"), depending on the specific aim of the role play. This is an excellent way to provide good data for post-session discussion.

5. Set up the scene. Label props, if any; show each participant where he or she should physically be and move to. A very brief introductory summary can help people get into the mood—"Mr. Smith, you're pretty annoyed at Joe, and you want to clear up this issue, now!" Make use of imagination—"This table will be a very big, classy executive desk." Few actual props are needed when imagination is effectively used.

6. Start the action. In multiple-group role playing it is helpful to have all groups start at the same time, on a signal.

7. Don't let the role play go on too long. While it is often desirable for each group in a multiple role play to reach a natural point of conclusion, slow groups should be pushed to finish and, eventually, simply stopped. When the role play is on stage, continuing is tempting, to see what will happen, but it is even more important in such cases to end as quickly as possible—when the problem is illustrated, when the point has been made, etc. Even a few minutes of an on-stage role play provides enough data for a thorough discussion; longer times overload the audience with information. It is also often useful to stop the action, discuss, and start again, either from the beginning, or with alternations ("pretend those last few sentences weren't said") or with advice for participants.

8. Debrief. Thank the role players, using their real names. For on-stage role playing this is important, because it returns the participants to their real identities. Discussion can then be far more objective and is less likely to hurt any of the role players. "Mr. Jones" may have made some bad mistakes, but Joe Blake, who played that role, doesn't have to feel bad for "Jones" errors.

9. Discuss what happened. The design of a discussion will depend very much on the specific situation and purpose of the role play. In general, the more views that are represented, the better. As in any discussion, the instructor or leader should try to keep the group on the right track without being too directive. When the multiple-group role-play procedure is used, discussion generally centers on comparison of outcomes, reports of observers (if any), and the feelings of participants about specific issues and behaviors. Some general guidelines for a discussion are:

    a. Determine what happened.

    b. Discuss what went well.

    c. Explore the reasons or causes for why the situation developed as it did and why the role players behaved as they did.

    d. Discuss how the outcome could have been better; what would the most desirable result have been. Why?

10. Repractice. A logical follow-up to 9d is to try out some of the actual behaviors that were suggested. This can be done on stage, and if so, a new group of role players may be desirable. Alternatively, the new behaviors can be tried out in multiple groups working simultaneously even if the model role play was on stage. Whenever role playing is used specifically as a skill practice exercise, it is desirable to repractice, often with roles reversed.

Unit 9
Making Your Own Better Meetings

We wish we could be with you as you discover and try out the many possible applications and adaptations of the ideas, tools, and designs we have shared with you. As you well know, good ideas do not automatically convert themselves into successful practice. It requires some trying out and development of specific skills. And, it is almost always a matter of personal adaptations to your own unique situation and personal style.

In its rough draft we found a number of ways to use this volume to help improve our meetings and those of others. These may be helpful to you:

1. We used it as a stimulus for ourselves, to discover alternative ideas before we decided on a particular design for a meeting, or conference, or class.
2. It was very helpful as a resource in consulting with the leaders of committees and staffs in helping them to improve their regular meetings.
3. We used it as a text for workshops and institutes on the designing of effective meetings for corporate, government, learning, and not-for-profit sector systems.
4. It was helpful with the program and planning committees of conferences and annual meetings.
5. In our work with organization development staffs in industry, business, and universities, it proved a very helpful resource.
6. It proved to be a stimulus in working with faculty groups on getting more participation and involvement into classroom teaching.
7. We found the ideas and resources helpful references in selecting instruments to duplicate or to modify for particular groups and persons.
8. It proved helpful as a resource for the many planners of organization programs who are seeking ways to make their meetings more interesting for their members, e.g., the Rotary Club, Junior League, Red Cross, Chamber of Commerce, boards of trustees, groups of managers, corporate presidents and vice presidents, professional associations, student leadership groups, etc.
9. Several groups of young people found it a help in improving the meetings of the student council, the Junior Achievement board, 4-H officers council, and others.

This is a sample of the uses we remember as we complete this volume for you.

One other tip: We keep two folders as supplements to this book. One folder is for the plans of meetings we have designed or helped design. The other folder contains copies of all the tools we have used in such meetings: start-up briefing sheets, evaluation sheets, feedback and stop-session tools, role-play instructions, etc.

We wish you good, productive, interesting, and involving meetings!

Bibliography

Auger, B.Y. (1972). *How to run better business meetings.* St. Paul, MN: Minnesota Mining and Manufacturing Company.

> Written by the general manager of the Visual Products Division of 3M. The contents are blueprints for turning any meeting into a productive experience. The material on visual aids is of particular help.

Haiku harvest (Japanese haiku series IV). (1962). (P. Beilenson & H. Behn, trans.). Mt. Vernon, NY: Peter Pauper.

> A lovely book of haiku poetry useful in starting or ending meetings. It also may be used to initiate philosophical discussions.

Benne, K., Bradford, L., Gibb, J., & Lippitt, R. (1975). *The laboratory method of learning and changing: Theory and applications.* Palo Alto, CA: Science & Behavior Books.

> The concept of the unstructured T-group and the beginnings of the laboratory method may properly be said to have started in 1946 when four leaders in education convened a workshop on intergroup relations at the State Teachers College in New Britain, Connecticut. Kenneth Benne, Leland Bradford, Ronald Lippitt, and Kurt Lewin originated those early concepts and methods, which since then have become diversified and spread into many institutional settings and into many parts of the world. The authors of this book have expanded on their earlier volume, *T-Group Theory and Laboratory Method,* often referred to as the "trainer's Bible." The newer book, destined to become another classic, is a quest for justifiable answers to the question "What is laboratory method?" This quest leads readers through a variety of theoretical discussions and evaluations of the method as well as descriptions of its practical applications in various human and institutional settings.

Benson, D. (1975). *Recycle catalogue.* Nashville, TN: Abingdon Press.

> A collection of 700 ways in which people working with groups and meetings have adapted ideas and materials for their groups.

Blanchard, K., & Lorber, R. (1984). *Putting the one minute manager to work: How to turn the 3 secrets into skills.* New York: William Morrow.

> Useful, simple, direct, and realistic hints on how to be an outstandingly effective manager, boss, or supervisor.

Burke, W.W., & Beckhard, R. (1976). *Conference planning* (2nd ed.). San Diego, CA: University Associates.

Much new material—including seven completely new articles—supplements and updates the first edition's thorough discussion of the basic principles of conference planning. A must for the planner, whether he is working on his first or twenty-fifth conference.

Business Education Division, Dun & Bradstreet, Inc. (1970). *How to conduct a meeting* (Dun & Bradstreet business series 9). New York: T.Y. Crowell.

A meeting can be a vital communication tool, and this book was written to help people make the most of this tool. It covers planning, arrangements, feelings of people, audience involvement, and tools for evaluation.

Daniels, W.R. (1986). *Group power: A manager's guide to using meetings.* San Diego, CA: University Associates.

A short (94-page) simple how-to-do-it guide for using meetings with a variety of techniques well described.

Didsbury, H.F., Jr. (Ed.). (1982). *Communications and the future: Prospects, promises, and problems.* Bethesda, MD: World Future Society.

A challenging and useful view of the future by a variety of experts. It includes topics such as communication, education, information, and instructional technology.

Dimock, H.G. (1987). *Groups: Leadership and group development.* San Diego, CA: University Associates.

An in-depth analysis of groups and how and why they function as they do.

Dutton, J.L. (1986). *How to be an outstanding speaker: Eight secrets to speaking success.* New London, WI: Life Skills.

A useful, helpful, clearly written instructional manual to help all to improve their presentation skills.

Finkel, C. (1972). *How to plan meetings like a professional.* Philadelphia, PA: S.M. Sales Meetings.

For persons responsible for planning larger meetings and those who are concerned with improving conference effectiveness.

Fletcher, W. (1983). *Meetings, meetings: How to manipulate them and make them more fun.* New York: William Morrow.

Ford, G.A., & Lippitt, G.L. (1976). *Planning your future: A workbook for personal goal setting.* San Diego, CA: University Associates.

A revision of the authors' earlier life-planning workbook, this is also a step-by-step workbook that guides the reader in planning and personal goal setting. It takes the individual through a sequence of tasks and exercises that aid in self-understanding and in planning both day-to-day and broad life goals more effectively.

Fox, R.S., Lippitt, R., & Schindler-Rainman, E. (1976). *The humanized future: Some new images* (Originally *Toward a humane society: Images of potentiality*). San Diego, CA: University Associates.

This book is particularly useful for meetings of which planning of future goals is the major purpose. It presents step-by-step designs to help a group move from formulating an image (a goal) to translating it into action.

Freas, S. (Ed.). (1985). *Meeting and event planning guide: Meeting sites and services directory, Southern California.* Santa Monica, CA: InterActive Publications.

A handy guide for places and spaces for meetings in Southern California.

Grove, A.S. (1983, July 11). How (and why) to run a meeting. *Fortune,* pp. 132-140.

The clear viewpoint of a business chief executive officer on what makes meetings cost effective, productive, and useful.

Hein, P. (1966, 1968, 1970, 1971, 1973). *Grooks 1, Grooks 2, Grooks 3, Grooks 4, Grooks 5.* New York: Doubleday.

These five amusing and delightful books are full of drawings and poetry (called Grooks) that are very useful as themes for meetings, as kickoff quotes, or as illustrations of points you wish to make. Each Grook captures some truth about the human condition as it is seen by the author, a Danish optimist writer and scientist.

Jay, A. (1976, March-April). How to run a meeting. *Harvard Business Review,* pp. 120-134.

Another view on meetings and the role of the meeting leader.

Jeffries, J.R. (1983). *The executive's guide to meetings, conferences, and audiovisual presentations.* New York: McGraw-Hill.

Josefowitz, N. (1980). *Paths to power: A women's guide from first job to top executive.* Reading, MA: Addison-Wesley.

One of the best and most explicit handbooks explaining power and how to understand and use it to influence others in socially acceptable ways.

Josefowitz, N. (1985). *You're the boss! A guide to managing people with understanding and effectiveness.* New York: Warner Books.

A wonderful book to give insights to all who want to understand, work with, and influence their bosses. It also helps bosses to be more effective in democratic ways.

Leslau, C., & Leslau, W. (1962). *African proverbs.* Mt. Vernon, NY: Peter Pauper.

Proverbs from all over Africa are delightfully apt for our culture and are useful as quotations.

Lippitt, G.L. (1976). *Visualizing change: Model building and the change process.* San Diego, CA: University Associates.

This volume shows how to picture or visualize the process of individual, group, or organizational change through the use of models.

Lippitt, G., & Lippitt, R. (1986). *The consulting process in action* (2nd ed.). San Diego, CA: University Associates.

The "bible" for consultants. It includes stages and phases of the internal and external consulting processes.

Maidment, R., & Bronstein, R. (1973). *Simulation games: Design and implementation.* Columbus, OH: Charles E. Merrill.

This is a short, helpful book covering simulations, simulation games, the history and uses of simulations, simulations and learning, and designing simulation games. It is a useful and informative book from which it is easy to adapt for different meetings and different purposes.

Manual for small meetings: Techniques to make small meetings produce results. (1975). Philadelphia, PA: Brill Communications.

A compendium of ideas, techniques, and procedures to help create and direct small meetings that are productive. Articles on leadership, participation, opening techniques, role playing, handling emergencies, and presentation techniques.

Morrisey, G. (1975). *Effective business and technical presentations* (2nd ed.). Reading, MA: Addison-Wesley.

Provides the reader with a step-by-step method, as well as practical exercises, to help ensure effective presentations. Also provides help on the selection and use of audiovisual aids and work sheets for planning, presenting, and evaluating presentations.

Mosvick, R.K., & Nelson, R.B. (1987). *We've got to start meeting like this! A guide to successful business meeting management.* San Diego, CA: University Associates.

This comprehensive book uses sample dialog from effective meetings, real-life experiences from survey respondents, and the opinions and theories of leading experts to help make these extraordinary concepts come alive.

Murray, P. (1970). *Dark testament and other poems.* Norwalk, CT: Silvermine.

This book reflects the author's Black experience from the 1930's through the late 1960's. It is a beautifully written book that can be used to involve group members in thinking and discussion; it is also very quotable.

O'Connell, B. (1985). *The board member's book.* New York: Foundation Center.

An excellent description and analysis of modern boards and how they should function realistically and productively.

Palmer, B.C. (1983). *The successful meeting master guide: For business and professional people.* Englewood Cliffs, NJ: Prentice-Hall.

Pfeiffer, J.W., Jones, J.E., & Goodstein, L.D. (Eds.). (1972-1988). The *Annual* series for HRD practitioners. San Diego, CA: University Associates.

Each of the *Annuals* contains new structured experiences, instruments, and professional development papers. A balanced variety of resources for program design and implementation.

Pfeiffer, J.W., & Jones, J.E. (Eds.). (1969, 1970, 1971, 1973, 1975, 1977, 1979, 1981, 1983, 1985). *A handbook of structured experiences for human relations training* (Vols. I-X). San Diego, CA: University Associates.

Each of the *Handbooks* contains activities that include useful methods, techniques, forms, questionnaires, and evaluations.

Research & Development Division, National Council of the Young Men's Christian Association. (1974). *Training volunteer leaders: A handbook to train volunteers and other leaders of program groups.* New York: Author.

This is a superb how-to-do-it tool for all persons who are concerned about improving the quality of leadership in groups. Over 100 exercises are described with helpful diagrams. Short essays on theory are strategically distributed to back up each exercise technique. Excellent for an extended training course; convenient for quick reference; useful in any setting.

Rudel & Finn, Inc. *18 conference room quotations and sculptures.* New York: American Institute of Graphic Arts.

This is a beautiful exhibit of quotations accompanied by pictures of famous sculptures. They can be used to motivate meeting participants either by exhibiting them selectively or by reading the quotations.

Schindler-Rainman, E. (1987) *The creative volunteer community: A collection of writings.* Vancouver, B.C., Canada: Voluntary Action Research Centre.

These collected writings span three decades and numerous subjects, yet they are knit together by recurrent key themes: the power of volunteer action; challenges and opportunities of change; appeal to creativity and collaboration.

Schindler-Rainman, E. (1981). Edited by Adolph, V. *Transitioning: strategies for the volunteer world.* Vancouver, B.C., Canada: Voluntary Action Research Centre.

Looks at changes in society, organizations, and individuals, and how those changes affect the volunteer field.

Schindler-Rainman, E., & Lippitt, R. (1975). *The volunteer community: Creative use of human resources* (2nd ed.). San Diego, CA: University Associates.

Two chapters in this book may be of particular interest to planners of meetings or conferences and trainers of trainers or staff. Chapter VII, "The Training of Trainers," deals with how to help trainees learn; it contains an illustrative trainership meeting design. Chapter IX illustrates interagency, community-wide planning meetings that evolve into a two-day community conference.

Schindler-Rainman, E., Lippitt, R., Millgate, I., & Olson, R. (1975). *Developing our volunteer community.* Tuxedo, NY: Xicom.

A package containing four programmed cassette tapes, a leader's manual, and *The Volunteer Community.* Designed to be used with any audiocassette recorder by any size group. Each section may be used separately or in a series of sessions. The package is structured as a professional development resource, a training device for staff, students, and volunteers, in small or large meetings, classes, conferences, or conventions.

Schindler-Rainman, E., & Lippitt, R. (1980). *Building the collaborative community: Mobilizing citizens for action.* Boulder, CO: Yellowfire.

A step-by-step explanation of a specific planning process.

This, L. (1972). *The small meeting planner.* Houston, TX: Gulf.

Designed for those who plan meetings, seminars, workshops, conferences, and training activities for 100 participants or less. Physical arrangements, table and chair constellations, and methods of evaluation are dealt with in depth.